The Gospel According to Paul

Volume 1
From God's No to God's Yes

Ronald E. Cottle, Ph.D, Ed.D
With David Alsobrook

Treasure House

An Imprint of
Destiny Image® Publishers, Inc.
P.O. Box 310
Shippensburg, PA 17257-0310

"For where your treasure is,
there will your heart be also." Matthew 6:21

ISBN 1-56043-282-9

For Worldwide Distribution
Printed in the U.S.A.

This book and all other Destiny Image, Revival Press, and Treasure House books are available at Christian bookstores and distributors worldwide.

For a U.S. bookstore nearest you, call **1-800-722-6774**. For more information on foreign distributors, call **717-532-3040**. Or reach us on the Internet: **http://www.reapernet.com**

Dedication

To Phil:

friend, colleague, encourager

Acknowledgments

Thanks to the thousands of students of Christian Life School of Theology who asked for and received these studies as lectures over the past decade. Their enthusiasm and many requests have led to the present book series.

Special thanks to my colleague and friend, David Alsobrook, whose assistance has given this book a quality of writing it could not have had without him.

Contents

Foreword. xi

Chapter 1   Nature, Background, and
Introduction to the Epistle. 1

Chapter 2   The Theme of Romans. 7

Chapter 3   Righteousness and Justification 27

Chapter 4   The Wrath of God 35

Chapter 5   Given Over by God. 45

Chapter 6   Taking Wrong Advantage
of God's Mercy 61

Chapter 7   Three Ways God
Will Judge Mankind 75

Chapter 8   The Faithfulness of God. 91

Chapter 9   Can a Person Go Too
Far to Be Saved? 99

Chapter 10   The Righteousness of God. 107

Epilogue 125

Foreword

*M*y publisher has presented an interesting challenge to me: to write a four-volume commentary on the Book of Romans. The volume you hold in your hands is the first. My division of Paul's Epistle to the Romans differs from the usual in some respects. I do not view chapter 4 of Romans as logically belonging in the first division of this biblical book. Instead, Paul's emphasis in chapters 1 through 3 is upon the wrath of God and its being overcome by His righteousness.

Chapter 4 of Romans, usually included in this first division, has not been left out, however. It appears with chapters 9, 10, and 11, as part of Paul's understanding—drawn logically from his earlier Book of Galatians—of the Church as the new, true Israel.

Thus Volume One focuses on the great transition from God's "no" to His "yes"—from wrath to righteousness through the Mercy Seat of Christ's cross. It concerns Romans 1:1–3:31.

Chapter 1

Nature, Background, and Introduction to the Epistle

*M*y purpose in writing this book is to give a study of the first three chapters of Romans that is more in-depth than most have read, but simple enough for the average person to understand. I love Romans more than any other book in the Bible, and I love the Bible more than any other book. S.W. Coleridge[1] complimented Romans as the "greatest written work in existence." I agree. Martin Luther subtitled Romans, "The Gospel According to Paul," which it indeed is. Of all Paul's letters, Romans comes nearest to being a theological treatise.

The nature of Romans is different from any other book Paul wrote. There is a different atmosphere and method here for two obvious reasons: 1) Paul did not

---

1. Cited by Spiros Zodhiates, *Hebrew-Greek Key Study Bible* (Chattanooga: AMG, 1984), 1366.

found the Church at Rome, hence, did not know anyone there; and he needed to set forth the gospel he preached in clear, concise, and unambiguous terms (the sixteenth chapter, scholarship agrees, actually belongs in Ephesians); 2) Paul did not have to correct any errors in doctrine or practice as he did with the Corinthians, the Galatians, and his other churches. As Martin Dibelius observed, "Romans is, of all Paul's letters, the least conditioned by the momentary situation."[2]

Paul's Objectives

Paul wrote this book in A.D. 58 while in Corinth after solving the problems of that church. Now, with his mind uncluttered, he had several objectives in view. First, he wanted to use this occasion as an opportunity to set forth God's program of salvation, setting forth his theological position in a systematic exposition. It's as if he propped his feet up and said, "Here's what I believe about the gospel." Because he was unaware of any immediate set of circumstances at Rome, he did not need to be pastoral in this letter; he could teach the gospel in all of its intricacies. This letter served as a personal introduction from Paul whose name they all knew. Now through it they would know both his heart and his gospel.

2. Cited by W. Barclay, *Romans, DSB* (Philadelphia: Westminster Press, 1955), XXI.

Second, Paul had a very practical reason for writing this letter. He desired to come to Rome, after this letter had paved the way of introduction, and minister among them for a season before heading toward Spain. From the earliest days of his conversion, having been told he would "stand before kings," Paul had longed to preach in the empire's capital. But he also wanted to go to Rome because he needed a new base of operations for the final phase of his ministry, which was the evangelization of Spain (see Acts 9:15; Rom. 15:24).

This would require the support of the Christians living closest to Western Europe, who happened to be located in the world's capital city. Years earlier Paul told the Ephesian Christians, "I must also see Rome" (Acts 19:21c). Jesus Himself appeared to Paul, when great opposition had arisen against him in Jerusalem, and promised, "You must also bear witness [of Me] at Rome" (Acts 23:11). Perhaps Paul felt that to strike at the very heart of the empire with the powerful gospel he preached was to deal a death blow to the spiritual stronghold of satan operating through Caesar. Paul was a visionary and a premier apostle, so it is almost certain that he entertained this idea; but his mentioned goal was to launch out from Rome westward into Europe.

Paul's burning desire was ever to preach the gospel in "the regions beyond" where Christ had not been named. Spain certainly qualified. Think of it...here was a man approaching his late fifties wanting to move to a different culture and learn a new language and do there what he had done throughout the Mediterranean world. Paul always had a goal; destiny was ever in his heart. He wanted to go forward to points where Christ was not known and there proclaim the gospel. Paul was a truly great man. He was known by face to more people than any other preacher in his day; but rather than rest on his laurels, his compassionate heart ever longed to reach more souls. The cause of Christ compelled him forward into labors more abundant.

William Barclay commented on his passion: "Paul was always haunted by the regions beyond. He never saw a ship at anchor, but he wished to board her, and to carry the message of the good news to the men across the sea. He never saw a range of mountains, but he wished to cross them to tell men of Jesus who have never heard."[3]

Rome would provide a strong base of support, both spiritual and financial, to help him fulfill this goal. Rome was to be Paul's Gilgal, his base of operations for ministry in Spain. "Whensoever I take my journey into Spain," he said, "...I trust...to be brought on my way [there] by you...I will come by you into Spain" (Rom. 15:24,28 KJV). In order to win their trust, the revered apostle of Asia Minor and Macedonia had first

---

3. Barclay, *Romans, DSB,* xxiii-xxiv.

to introduce himself and establish a relationship with these saints.

Prior to accomplishing his intended mission to Spain, Paul had a service to fulfill to the Christians suffering extreme famine in Judea. He had received a very large offering from the churches under his oversight; and since the day it had been entrusted to his care, Paul wished to transport this almsgift to "the poor saints in Jerusalem." But there were rabid Jewish zealots throughout Palestine still plotting his death; and recognizing his need of divine protection, he requested the spiritual support of the believers in Rome that they would "strive together with [him] in [their] prayers to God for [him in order that he would] be delivered from them that do not believe..." (Rom. 15:30b-31 KJV).

Paul's third objective in writing was to set the stage for him to minister directly to these believers. He yearned to impart a spiritual gift to them and establish them deeper in their faith (see Rom. 1:11). He would accomplish this first, by means of this letter, and second, by means of his personal ministry among them. "So, as much as is in me, I am ready to preach the gospel to you who are in Rome also" (Rom. 1:15).

Chapter 2

The Theme of Romans

The theme of Romans is "the gospel according to Paul," which is salvation by faith:

For I am not ashamed of the gospel of Christ, for it is the power of God to salvation for everyone who believes, for the Jew first and also for the Greek (Romans 1:16).

This theme is not restricted to salvation but is expanded to all of life: "The just shall live by faith" (Rom. 1:17b). One rendering of the original reads, "the just by faith shall live by faith," meaning that a person is made just (righteous) by faith and then continues living by faith.

The first 17 verses of the book serve as the introduction. The first seven contain the address and salutation. For convenience' sake, we will examine them one verse at a time.

Paul, a bondservant of Jesus Christ, called to be an apostle, separated to the gospel of God (Romans 1:1).

From Saul to Paul

As was his custom in all his letters, Paul identifies himself at the outset. There is no little confusion regarding the name of this beloved apostle. In Sunday schools it is often said that Saul became Paul, dropping the "S" and adding the "P" to denote his conversion. This is humorous and completely untrue. In the original languages these two names do not rhyme or even sound close. The Greek word *Paulos* is not the translation of the Hebrew word *Sha'al*. They are not even close in meaning. J.D. Douglas says that Saul is the Jewish name of Paul (*The New Bible Dictionary*). This is, at best, misleading, although it is true that it was not uncommon for a Jew to take a Greek name for business purposes in the Gentile world. Undoubtedly, this was part of the reason for the name change; however, there is something far deeper in the name change of this unique man.

Sha'al means "asked of God." His parents were God-fearing Jews who had obviously prayed for a son and whose prayers had been graciously answered. Out of gratitude they named their little boy Saul because he had been asked of God. *Paulos* comes from *pauo* and means "to cease, restrain, diminish." (Our English word *pause* comes from this root.) Saul of Tarsus was a madman just prior to his conversion. He persecuted the early Church with vehemence and zeal. He needed to be stopped.

One day, enroute to Damascus, this revered Pharisee was apprehended by God. Sprawled flat in the dirt he was confronted with the very One he was persecuting. His religious training had instilled the belief that God is light, and this One appeared in a Light that caused the bright midday sun to pale (see Acts 26:13). Later Paul would write that Jesus dwells in unapproachable light (see 1 Tim. 6:16). "Who are You, Lord?" he asked in his daze. "I am Jesus..." the Brilliant One answered (Acts 9:5). This caused Saul to pause (to cease, restrain, and diminish) his activities for three days while he and his burned retinas contemplated his faulty belief system. This divine intervention resulted in a complete life change.

He is first called Paul in Acts 13:9, years after his conversion, during his first missionary journey with Barnabas. It is probable that he did not take this name for himself, but was given this name by Christian friends in Antioch who had witnessed the revolution of a murderous persecutor into a magnificent proclaimer of Christ. Saul came to the end of himself on the Damascus road and was transformed into Paul.

A Bondservant of Jesus Christ

The Greek is interesting here: *doulos Iesou Christou.* *Doulos* (1491) means "servant, slave." It is the Greek translation of the Hebrew word *ebed,* which referred to the Old Testament bond slave, rather than the hired slave. Exodus 21:1-11 shows the striking differences between the two types of slaves allowed under the Law.

The *ebed* served his master forever out of willingness; he was not forced. It is interesting to notice that the Hebrew Scriptures refer to Moses, Abraham, Jeremiah, and virtually every other major character as an *ebed Yahweh* (bond slave of Jehovah). In the New Testament, Paul, Peter, James, John, and Jude all referred to themselves as "bond slaves of Jesus Christ." (*Doulos* is more correctly rendered "slave" than "servant.") All of these believers were designating Jesus Christ as absolute owner and master of their lives by employing this term. "I am the slave of Jesus," they were boasting. "If He wants me to live, I will live. If He wants me to die, I will die. Whatever He wants, I want." Oh, what highest honor, to be a bond slave of Christ!

Called *to Be* an Apostle

The word for "called" is *kletos* and means "called one." It comes from the word *kallein,* which means "to call." We sometimes fail to grasp the significance of this word, however, because of our informal language. We call one another on the telephone or call our family to dinner. In Paul's day, the word meant far more than an invitation. It is a strong word that we could compare to a legal summons (as in being called or declared "not guilty" by a court). It is the equivalent of the Hebrew word *qara'* where "God *called* the light Day, and the darkness He *called* Night" (Gen. 1:5a). It is a command word that creates what it says. You are what God *calls* you.

The word for "church" also comes from this same root. It is *ekklesia* and means "called-out ones." We were not merely invited to Jesus; we were summoned to Him, called out from the world, and created sons and daughters of God by His call.

William Hollar Hunt painted the famous "Christ Standing at the Door," which I am sure you have seen. He depicted Jesus in the style of his day—an effeminate-looking man with long, flowing locks gently tapping on a European-style door.

Karl Barth was gloriously converted during World War I when a bomb demolished his church; and when someone commented to him that Hunt's work was the greatest work of Christian art in the decade, it is said that Barth tersely replied, "Neine, neine, neine!" Then he explained, "When Jesus called me He did not stand like an effeminate one, gently tapping at my door asking me in my power to let Him in out of the elements. Instead, He came stripped, bruised, and bleeding, and took the big end of a bloody cross and with it He banged against the door of my resisting heart. When I could not stand the banging any longer, I quit standing against the door to shut Him out. Then He tore the door of my resistance off its hinges, walked into the citadel of my heart, and crowned Himself King of my life."

Barth's response is a truer description of the God who calls than the popular concept of a God who is begging, "Oh, won't you please accept Me?" He commands us to come. This is the way God called Paul, Barth, and you. He has summoned you to Himself and changed your life by that call. "Old things have passed away; behold, all things have become new" (2 Cor. 5:17b). "Blessed is the man You choose, and cause to approach You, that he may dwell in Your courts" (Ps. 65:4a).

In Romans 1:11 the words "to be" are in italics, which indicates that they were supplied by the translators, not part of the original text. This phrase does a great disservice to Paul's intention. He was not called to become an apostle; he was called an apostle. When God called Paul "apostle," that is what made him such. It is the difference between becoming something by one's own will and effort and being made something by God's will, Word, and effort. *When God calls you, He makes you whatever it is He calls you.* The secret to happiness in life is being and doing what you are. This calling took place when God separated the apostle from his mother's womb (see Gal. 1:15).

Apostle is *apostolos* or "apostled one." The original meaning is important for our understanding: *apo* means "from" and *stellos* is the Greek equivalent of the Hebrew word *shalach* (sent), which is the original root for *mashiach* or Messiah! This is why Jesus is the chief apostle (see Heb. 3:1). *It means far more than the common definition of a "sent one."* All ministry gifts are sent ones, but the apostle is the "one sent with the plenary authority of the Sender." In other words, *he is sent in order to send others.* An apostle is God's delegated authority, His ambassador or legal representative for a city or community. The apostle raises up churches and leaders and sends them forth with his authority to raise up more churches and leaders. The idea hails back to Genesis 24 where Abraham's servant, having put his hand under Abraham's thigh (the place of his seed), is sent to Nahor with the authority of Abraham. Eliezer sits at their table, a mere slave, and speaks with the authority of a ruler. They listen to Eliezer *as though he were Abraham* for he is Abraham's delegated authority.

Separated to the Gospel of God

Paul is fond of using words which have deeper meaning. In Romans 1:1 the word for "separated" is *aphorismenos* and means "set apart one," but the term is actually a play on the word "Pharisee"! Thus, Paul is alluding back to his origin when he was separated to the Pharisee sect even as a boy. His parents trained him in the Torah, which he knew by heart at age six, and the

Psalms and Prophets, which he had memorized by age 12. The Pharisees were the strictest sect of Judaism, and Saul of Tarsus was one of their most devoted adherents. But now he was set apart to the gospel.

This root is used three times of Paul—in Galatians 1:15 where God separated him by His sovereign choice, in Acts 13:2 where the church separated him by a word of knowledge, and in Romans 1:1 where Paul separated himself by his personal consecration. This bond slave of Jesus was a separated one to His gospel. The word for "gospel" is *euaggelion* (the evangel) and came to mean primarily "the written gospel." But there was one before that.

The Earliest Gospel

The *Kerygma* (pronounced: kay-rig-mah) is that term which refers to the earliest gospel, the vocal gospel. The vocal gospel began with Jesus, even as Hebrews 2:3 confirms that our great salvation "first began to be spoken by the Lord." This was about A.D. 30. The *Kerygma* continued until A.D. 66 when Mark wrote the first Gospel, also known as the *Evangel*.

Life precedes literature; we must experience something before we can write its history. The gospel that was preached from the time of Jesus until Mark's Gospel, the *Kerygma*, is the gospel everyone preached before the New Testament was written.

What is the *Kerygma* and where can we find it in the Scriptures? In 1926 Charles Harold Dodd wrote a small book titled *The Apostolic Preaching and Its Developments.*[1] Dodd found three places in the New Testament containing the *Kerygma*—that which the disciples preached prior to the writing of the New Testament. One of the three places is Romans 1:2-4.

The *Kerygma* in Romans contains five major points:

1. Jesus Christ was prophesied in the Holy Scriptures:

> *Which He promised before through His prophets in the Holy Scriptures* (Romans 1:2).

During the first three decades of the Church, the early evangelists went forth with the Septuagint, the Greek translation of the Hebrew Old Testament, and preached Jesus from Genesis to Malachi.

2. Jesus was incarnated.

> *Concerning His Son Jesus Christ our Lord, who was born of the seed of David according to the flesh* (Romans 1:3).

This is not one of the primary Incarnation texts, but it is here. The early evangelists stressed the truth that God became man.

3. Jesus was resurrected.

> *And declared to be the Son of God with power according to the Spirit of holiness, by the resurrection from the dead* (Romans 1:4).

---

1. C.H. Dodd, *The Apostolic Preaching and Its Developments* (Cambridge: Hodder and Stoughton, 1936).

Every sermon in the Book of Acts included the resurrection of Christ. Every book of the New Testament, with the exception of James, includes Christ's resurrection. The early evangelists heralded the resurrection as part of their regular preaching. The resurrection validates the crucifixion and, hence, Christ's atonement claims.

4. Jesus has sent forth representatives.

> *Through Him we have received grace and apostleship for obedience to the faith among all nations for His name* (Romans 1:5).

The early evangelists were the representatives of Christ Himself to those to whom they were sent.

5. Jesus has called us His own.

> *Among whom you also are the called of Jesus Christ* (Romans 1:6).

Jesus is gathering His people through repentance and belief on His work.

Points 4 and 5 above are not as fundamental as points 1, 2, and 3. When we look at the other two *Kerygma* passages, we see the same points emphasized—that Christ was prophesied, crucified, and resurrected (see Acts 2:22-36; 1 Cor. 15:3-9). This was the core of early preaching. Christ was prophesied in the Old Testament; He came by virgin birth to man; He was crucified by wicked hands, but resurrected by divine power.

A lot of what we hear preached today rarely touches on these points, but the earliest representatives of Jesus Christ emphasized them every time they preached. The *Kerygma* is still the essence of the gospel.

What is true preaching? It is proclaiming the gospel which belongs to Jesus Christ—His incarnation, sinless life, vicarious death, resurrection, and ascension. True preaching is not just imparting truth, not even truth about God. *True preaching is bringing about an encounter between God and man from which man will never be the same!* This makes one wonder how much true preaching is done today.

Salutation

Among whom you also are the called of Jesus Christ; to all who are in Rome, beloved of God, called to be saints: Grace to you and peace from God our Father and the Lord Jesus Christ (Romans 1:6-7).

Having declared his own calling, Paul now turns to the believers at Rome and acknowledges their calling. "You are also *kletos*," he tells them, "the called" by Jesus Christ. They are "beloved of God" because of this calling and are "called *to be* saints," which actually says in the Greek "called saints." Sainthood is not something these Romans are called to possess by their own efforts, but something they already possess because God called them saints.

The word study on "saints" is most interesting. It is the Greek word *hagios* (separated to God), which is the opposite of *anathema* (separated from God). Both of these words are derived from the Hebrew word *herem* from which the word "harem" is derived!

The special significance of *hagios* now comes into view. Just as all the females in a harem are devoted to one person, those who are saints are devoted to Yahweh's pleasure alone. We are the Bride of Christ, the *herem Yahweh*! On the opposite side, those who are *anathema* are cursed, devoted to destruction—in short, the damned, those devoted to satan's pleasure.

"Grace and peace," Paul declares to these saints, following the same pattern of blessing as in all his epistles. It is interesting that Paul never reverses the words. That is because we can only know peace through God's grace. We should understand that this was more than a mere greeting—it was an apostolic blessing.

Thanksgiving

First, I thank my God through Jesus Christ for you all, that your faith is spoken of throughout the whole world. For God is my witness, whom I serve with my spirit in the gospel of His Son, that without ceasing I make mention of you always in my prayers, making request if, by some means, now at last I may find a way in the will of God to come to you. For I long to see you, that I may impart to you some spiritual gift, so that you may be established—that is, that I may be encouraged together with you by the mutual faith both of you and me. Now I do not want you to be unaware, brethren, that I often planned to come to you (but was hindered until now), that I might have some fruit among you also, just as among other Gentiles. I am a debtor both to Greeks and to barbarians, both to wise and to unwise. So, as much as is in me, I am ready to preach the gospel to you who are in Rome also (Romans 1:8-15).

Paul begins with the word "first" in verse 8. The word is *proton* and means "first in a line of successive things," much like a prototype in an assembly plant. Paul has many things for which to be thankful, the first of which is their faith. This is the word *pistis* and is the single most important word in Romans. We will examine it a few verses later, but for now we should notice that the church at Rome was famous throughout the whole world for its faith in Christ. (The phrase "is spoken about" is *kataggelo* and means "famous." "Throughout the whole world" is *holo' to' kosmo'* and means "throughout the Roman Empire.")

This is a church Paul has yet to meet, but the believers there are ever in his prayers, even to the point of praying "without ceasing" for them. This is *adialeiptos* and means "without interruption, omission, and intermission." Rome was a part of Paul's permanent prayer life, partly perhaps because of their strategic location.

Paul "longs to see" these saints. The word for "long" is *epipotheo'*, which means "to yearn, to desire greatly." Paul has a deep desire to go to Rome, for reasons we discussed in Chapter 1, but also because he yearns to "impart...some spiritual gift" to them that will make them ever more "established." The word for "impart" is *metadidomi* and means "to give, share, impart, distribute, grant." The word implies liberality or generosity. The word for "gift" is *charisma* and refers to a "grace portion," which he longs to share, a deposit he wishes to make into that church.

Paul then adds that he knows he will be "encouraged together with" them through mutual sharing, and that he had planned to come to Rome earlier, but was hindered in doing so. Because he was the apostle to the Gentiles, he had a divine right to fruit among them, as "among the other Gentiles."

Then, Paul gave his classic statement that has become an inspirational text to every missionary since:

I am a debtor both to Greeks and to barbarians, both to wise and to unwise. So, as much as is in me, I am ready to preach the gospel to you who are in Rome also (Romans 1:14-15).

The word "debtor" (*opheiletes*) means both "I owe" and "I ought." Paul owed a debt of the gospel to everyone because he had received the benefits of the same. Does this grip your heart? It should. He was "ready" (*prothumos*), which means he felt intensely with a great desire toward them to discharge the gospel of Christ.

The Theme of the Book

This brings us to the salvation theme of Romans: *the gospel is power!*

> For I am not ashamed of the gospel of Christ, for it is the power of God to salvation for everyone who believes, for the Jew first and also for the Greek. For in it the righteousness of God is revealed from faith to faith; as it is written, "The just shall live by faith" (Romans 1:16-17).

The term "gospel of Christ" is the same as the term "gospel of God." Both terms mean "the gospel which belongs to Christ and God." Paul declared, "the gospel of Christ...is the power of God to salvation." The phrase "power of God" is *dunamis Theou* and means "the released energy of God." The gospel is power! Power "to salvation" (*eis soterian*) means "for the purpose of, or into, deliverance, wholeness, and preservation." In every generation people are looking for reality. The gospel is that for which they search.

There were many "gospels" in this period of history, many who preached salvation by one means or another. Let me explain. In Paul's day men sought one thing above all else in life—salvation. It was believed that a horrible fate controlled the world and the destinies of men. Therefore, philosophers of Paul's day and those a century before concentrated upon building a wall of defense against the advancing chaos of the world.

The fringe Jewish groups of the Dead Sea area including the Essenes, the group from which John the Baptist probably came, resorted to multiple baptisms—literally baptisms for virtually everything—hoping to cleanse their souls.

The mainline Judaists resorted to keeping laws and multiplying them. The Mishna laws contained over 2,000 additional commandments amplifying the Mosaic requirements. There occurred what Arnold Toynbee called "a loss of nerve" in the first century B.C. The world felt itself "crumbling to pieces," he said.

Epictetus, a Greek philosopher of this period, called his lecture room "the hospital for the sick soul." Epicurus, founder of Epicureanism, called his philosophy, "the medicine of salvation." Seneca, the leading philosopher of Rome during Paul's lifetime, said, *"All men are looking for salvation. What we need is a hand to lift us up."*

Here Paul answers the very heart cry of the people of Rome with the gospel of Christ. The answer to man's yearning heart, he said, is the gospel of Christ—God's power to salvation! Paul presented a twofold application:

1. Salvation (wholeness) in life.

   > *...In all things God is at work for good to them who love Him...* (Romans 8:28, literal).

   > *For I am persuaded that neither death nor life...nor things present nor things to come... shall be able to separate us from the love of*

God which is in Christ Jesus our Lord (Romans 8:38).

2. Salvation (safety) in death.

Rupert Brooke wrote:

> Safe shall be my going,
> Secretly armed against all death's endeavor;
> Safe though all safety's lost; safe where men fall;
> And if these poor limbs die; safest of all.[2]

Robert Browning adds:

> If I stoop
> Into a dark tremendous sea of cloud,
> It is but for a time; I press God's lamp
> Close to my breast; its splendor sooner or later,
> Will pierce the gloom: I shall emerge one day.[3]

In Paul's concept of salvation, he saw a salvation in Christ that made a man safe in such a way that is independent of and above all circumstances! Paul's "salvation" (*soteria*) is equivalent to John's "life" (*zoe*). Both are the result of the power of God that encounters man in and through the gospel.

For Everyone Who Believes

With this statement, we have arrived at the *key* to this epistle. The word "faith" (*pistis*), which occurs here

2. Barclay, *Romans, DSB*, 11.
3. Barclay, *Romans, DSB*, 11.

in a verb form (believes) and in verse 17 in a noun form (faith), unlocks the door to Paul's mind and theology— the theology that swept the ancient world and is still the best vehicle of Christ's gospel today. *Faith is the key to salvation.*

Paul used this word three times in his introduction (verses 5,8,12) and four times in verses 16 and 17. What does Paul mean when he says "faith"? If we learn the answer to that question, we will enter into a place of blessed rest with God.

There are several legitimate meanings of faith in the writings of Paul:

1. Loyalty or faithfulness.

   So that we ourselves boast of you among the churches of God for your patience and faith in all your persecutions and tribulations that you endure (2 Thessalonians 1:4).

2. Belief.

   And if Christ is not risen, your faith is futile; you are still in your sins! (1 Corinthians 15:17)

3. The Christian religion.

   Examine yourselves as to whether you are in the faith. (2 Corinthians 13:5a).

4. Absolute trust and total acceptance.

   ...it is the power of God to salvation for everyone who believes... (Romans 1:16).

Paul's faith in this passage is absolute trust, the kind that stakes everything for time and eternity on Jesus Christ. It is betting your life on Jesus! Robert Louis Stevenson expressed it this way: "I believe in God, and even if I woke up in hell I would still believe in Him."

There are three basic elements of saving faith: 1) *Acknowledgment*—This occurs when one recognizes with the mind the truth of one's state and Christ's sufficiency; 2) *Acceptance*—This happens when repentance takes place in the heart; 3) *Appropriation*—This takes place when one returns his will to God's desires. When these three elements are present, one is truly regenerated or born again. Any "faith" less than this cannot please God (see Heb. 11:6). This is what conversion is all about—turning around and going in the opposite direction.

Paul's faith involves the total man. It necessitates action and will. It may be said that "Faith is the will leaping forth to embrace and appropriate the Christ whom the mind has come to know and trust."

It's easy to see how little the average churchgoer understands true faith in our day, isn't it? All too often we are merely professors of faith rather than possessors of it. I believe our weak, anemic faith, if it is faith at all, is the root of many of our problems in the church today. May God bring us all into real faith so that we can experience the power of the gospel of Christ—the kind of power that releases divine energy into our lives, transforming us from darkness to light!

In Chapter 3 we will look at the remainder of verse 17 and focus on "the righteousness of God." As we saw with faith, we will understand anew what Paul meant when he said, "The just [righteous] will live by faith."

Chapter 3

Righteousness and Justification

or I am not ashamed of the gospel of Christ, for it is the power of God to salvation for everyone who believes, for the Jew first and also for the Greek. For in it the righteousness of God is revealed from faith to faith; as it is written, "The just shall live by faith" (Romans 1:16-17).

Righteousness and Faith

We now come to the heart of Romans and, indeed, of the entire gospel. Our central phrase is "the righteousness of God." This righteousness of God is revealed in the gospel of Christ, which is "the power of God to salvation for everyone who believes, for the Jew first and also for the Greek."

The phrase "for the Jew first and also for the Greek," I am convinced, has historical, rather than theological, significance, as the gospel was proclaimed to the adherents of Judaism before it was proclaimed to Gentiles. What Paul means in this phrase is that the gospel is universal in both its appeal and power. (The word Paul used for "first" is *proton,* which means first in a line of things, rather than *archon,* which means "first in priority or importance.")

But what does "the righteousness of God" refer to? F.F. Bruce, in his commentary on Romans, says:

"Righteousness is to the Hebrew not so much a moral quality as a legal status."[1]

Paul equates righteousness with justification and William Barclay commented, "There are no more difficult words in all the New Testament to understand than justification, justify, justice, and just."[2]

We must understand, first of all, that the word "justify" in English is not at all what the New Testament means by the term. In the English sense, when we justify ourselves we produce reasons to prove we are right, but in the Greek sense we mean to treat, account, or reckon a person to be something he is not, in or by himself. The verb *dikaioo* ends in *oo* and never means to *prove* or even *make* a person or thing into something else, but to treat a person or thing *as* something else!

1. F.F. Bruce, *The Letter of Paul to the Romans* (Grand Rapids: William B. Eerdmans, 1985), rev. ed., 73; emphasis mine.
2. Barclay, *Romans, DSB,* 13.

When God justifies a sinner, it does not mean that He finds reasons in that sinner to prove that the sinner is right...far from it! Neither does it mean (at the point of justification) that God makes the sinner a good person. What it does mean is that God treats the sinner as if he had never sinned at all! Instead of viewing him as a criminal to be destroyed, God treats him as a child to be loved. God treats us not as bad men deserve, but as good men deserve. This is what justification means and is the reason why English scholars made the famous play on the word "justified" into "just-as-if-I'd" never sinned.

Justification occurs when God declares a person legally righteous. When God justifies us, He changes not us, but the relationship between Himself and us.

This is the true meaning of justification. A just man is one who is in right relationship with God. And here is the wonderful truth about it all...a just man is in this right relationship with God, *not through anything he himself has done, but because of that which God has done!*

This is why a just man can declare, "I am saved and delivered out of all my sinful bondage, not because of what I did, but because of what He did, not even because of what I became, but because of Who He is!"

Of course, no one could be justified had justice not been served, and it was fully served upon Jesus at Golgotha's hill. It is very important that we understand this.

And then it is this close relationship of love and trust between us and our Creator, by which God transforms us in progressive sanctifying power to actually change us into new creatures. *Christianity is becoming who we are by virtue of what God calls us.* But God calls us righteous before any change in our lives occurs. This is why we need to be very patient with new converts. They have things to overcome that they took years to develop, and may take years to change, but they are righteous the moment they believe on Christ.

I was raised in an extremely legalistic form of Christianity. It wasn't until I was a seminarian that this truth burst upon me in those quiet halls. I wanted to shout, and I did inside, when I saw, through the Reformer's teachings, the truth of justification. I am not saying that everyone in that Lutheran seminary saw what I did, but Luther and his contemporaries taught me something I had never seen before, and the truth liberated me from drowning in the dangerous waters of legalism. We are righteous simply because God says so.

The righteousness of God is revealed to us "from faith to faith" (*ek pisteos eis pistin*), not simply a righteousness, but *the very righteousness of God* is given us by faith (see 2 Cor. 5:21). On man's side, salvation is completely a matter of faith from start to finish:

Faith is a gift of God received in utter submission:

For by grace you have been saved through faith, and that not of yourselves; it is the gift of God, not of works, lest anyone should boast (Ephesians 2:8-9).

In this text Paul tells us that the faith by which saving grace comes to us is the gift of God. The word he used for "gift" in verse 8 is *doron* and means a present given without strings attached to it. In other words, it is yours to use in any manner you wish, a bona fide gift. This gift is received into the repentant heart while in utter submission to the Savior.

Faith is an attitude of the whole life:

I have been crucified with Christ; it is no longer I who live, but Christ lives in me; and the life which I now live in the flesh I live by faith in the Son of God, who loved me and gave Himself for me (Galatians 2:20).

The word for "life" in this text is not *bios* (human, physical, natural life) but *zoe* (divine life). Paul says, "the *zoe* which I now *zoe* I *zoe* by faith in the Son of God." Divine life is received and continued in by faith.

Faith is a creative, ethical force:

*And though I have **the gift** of prophecy, and understand all mysteries and all knowledge, and though I have all faith, so that I could remove mountains, but have not love, I am nothing* (1 Corinthians 13:2).

In this verse the apostle shows us that faith is an ethic predicated by love. Without *agape* controlling me, I am nothing, even though I may have the creative force of faith sufficient to alter nature.

The Just by Faith Shall Live by Faith

Paul now proceeds to amplify the subject of faith, showing that we are made just by faith and then continue our new life by faith. He quotes a verse from the prophet Habakkuk:

Behold the proud, his soul is not upright in him; but the just shall live by his faith (Habakkuk 2:4).

Habakkuk's meaning is clear from the context: a righteous man will come through the storms of life by virtue of his faithfulness to God and Israel.

Paul, on the other hand, means something essentially different: *he who, by faith, is righteous shall live by faith.* This is the practical theme of Romans and the scriptural text upon which Paul preaches the gospel in this book. (Paul also quotes Habakkuk 2:4 in Galatians 3:11 where he refutes legalism.) In fact, Romans falls into four divisions on the basis of this text, which is my writing plan for everything I am preparing for you, the reader.

The phrase, "the just shall live by faith," actually says, "the just by faith shall live by faith," as I pointed out in the previous chapter. Once again, it is imperative that we understand that we are righteous (just) by faith, not by anything else ("not of works, lest anyone should boast") and that we continue living before God upon the same basis. This truth is woven into the tapestry of Romans 1:18–3:31, so we need to engrave it upon our hearts as the threads of this truth run throughout the remainder of this volume.

We do not become righteous by faith to thereafter live by works. The man who is righteous by faith continues to live by faith. Nothing else can please God (see Heb. 11:6). Having begun in the Spirit, we will never be made perfect by the flesh, no matter how "good" that flesh is (see Gal. 3:3)! No, we continue as we began: "As you therefore have received Christ Jesus the Lord, so walk in Him" (Col. 2:6). We keep it like we got it—by faith.

There is only one alternative to the righteousness of God and that is the theme of our next chapter.

Chapter 4

The Wrath of God

or the wrath of God is revealed from heaven against all ungodliness and unrighteousness of men, who suppress the truth in unrighteousness, because what may be known of God is manifest in them, for God has shown it to them. For since the creation of the world His invisible attributes are clearly seen, being understood by the things that are made, even His eternal power and Godhead, so that they are without excuse, because, although they knew God, they did not glorify Him as God, nor were thankful, but became futile in their thoughts, and their foolish hearts were darkened. Professing to be wise, they became fools, and changed the glory of the incorruptible God into an image made like corruptible man—and birds and four-footed animals and creeping things (Romans 1:18-23).

In the preceding chapter we saw the relationship between a man and God when there is trust and commitment (true faith). Paul now contrasts that blessed relationship with that of a man who is deliberately blind to God and who worships himself as his own idol, or debases himself even lower to worship lesser creatures. This relationship is called "the wrath of God." It is a horrible and terrifying concept and one that did not originate with Paul, although he elevated it to its highest understanding. There are three stages in the development of man's understanding of the wrath of God in the Word. The first stage came through Moses, the second stage through the Prophets, and the final stage through Paul. Let's look at the development of wrath in the Scriptures.

The Mosaic Tradition: *Wrath Is an Emotion*

Wrath first appears in the pre-prophetic tradition of the Old Testament where it is especially connected with the covenant people of God through the ministry of Moses. The *Torah* (or Pentateuch as Protestants call it) reveals that Israel had a special relationship with God based upon love. God was seen as a jealous husband and Israel was His bride. This love in the Hebrew is the special word *chesed* and can be defined as "merciful trust."

> *So Moses came and told the people all the words of the Lord and all the judgments. And all the people answered with one voice and said, "All the words which the Lord has said we will do." ... And Moses took the*

blood, sprinkled it on the people, and said, "This is the blood of the covenant which the Lord has made with you according to all these words" (Exodus 24:3,8).

This relationship remained inviolate as long as God's ancient people kept His Law. Obedience to the Law of God, as given through His *ebed Yahweh*, Moses, was the prerequisite for avoiding God's jealous wrath. This meant two things:

1. *Any breaking of God's Law brought His wrath.*

In Numbers 16:46 (KJV) we are told of God's wrath that came upon Israel due to the rebellion of Korah: "...*there is wrath gone out from the Lord....*" When the covenant people were led astray into Baal worship, "the anger of the Lord was kindled against Israel" (Num. 25:3 KJV).

Because Israel had a special relationship with God, any breach of His trust brought His wrath, as the unfaithfulness of a wife might bring the jealous response of a betrayed husband.

2. *Any nation that oppressed Israel brought God's wrath upon themselves.*

When Moses led Israel through the wilderness, God punished kings for their sakes (see Ps. 105:14). When they were led, under Joshua, "from one nation to another" in Canaan, "He permitted no man to do them wrong...saying, 'Do not touch My anointed ones, and do My prophets no harm' " (1 Chron. 16:20-22). The jealous Yahweh was protecting His betrothed.

Later, in the Prophetic Period, this wrath was displayed against Assyria and Babylon for the same reason. These nations had powerful armies that were actually used by Yahweh, as strange as that may sound, to administer His discipline to wayward Israel at two different times in her history. Yet, after God used "the rod of [His] anger" (His term for Assyria), He turned around and punished that nation for their willing persecution of Israel and their egotism (see Is. 10:5-11).

In like manner, ancient Babylon was used to chasten Israel for polluting the promised land with idolatry and other sins. God purposed 70 years of captivity in that strange land; but the Babylonian forces were especially cruel to God's covenant people, so Yahweh promised Babylon "shall not be inhabited," even as Israel had been temporarily evacuated, as a result of their cruelty (see Jer. 50:13).

In the Mosaic understanding of the wrath of God, we see His wrath displayed as *emotional anger*, which is never the way His wrath is viewed in the New Testament, as we shall see.

God does not change, but our perceptions of Him change as we grow in understanding. When I was first saved at age 14, God was my "sugar daddy"—He gave me everything I wanted. By the time I was 16, He was my stern Judge, before whom I cringed in terrified, legalistic obedience. Now, after all these years of coming to know Him, He has become a true Father to me in every sense of the word and my very best Friend. But God is the same now as He was all those years ago. He hasn't changed, but my perception of Him has changed as a result of my growth.

Under the Law, Israel trembled in fear of God's emotional anger and asked that He not speak with them directly anymore. Even Moses quaked with exceeding fear (see Heb. 12:18-21). How different this is from a loving Father we reverence with a godly fear, but not a shrinking terror.

The Prophetic Period: *Wrath Is a Possession*

The concept of the wrath of God developed another emphasis in the Prophets of the Old Testament. Instead of being merely the anger of God against sin, wrath became *the automatic annihilating reaction of God toward sin.*

After the death of the prophet Samuel, Uzzah stretched forth his hand to steady the Ark and was immediately executed (see 2 Sam. 6:6-8). This is only one example of automatic annihilation.

R.C.H. Lenski says, "This wrath is not fiction nor a figure of speech, but a terrible reality, the constant unchanging reaction of God's holiness and righteousness to sin. ... Because God is God, and because God is characteristically holy, God cannot tolerate sin and the wrath of God is God's reaction against sin."[1]

The Prophets also gave a future application to God's wrath when they foresaw "a great and terrible time" called "the day of the LORD" (see Joel 2:11,31; Zeph. 2:11). This was to be "a day of clouds and darkness" that would bring retribution and judgment to the enemies of Yahweh (see Amos 5:18). "That day is a day of wrath, a day of trouble and distress" (Zeph. 1:15a). Isaiah saw it clearly: "Behold, the day of the Lord comes, cruel, with both wrath and fierce anger, to lay the land desolate; and He will destroy its sinners from it" (Is. 13:9). Thus, the Prophets foresaw the judgment of God upon the earth in the last days and even His eternal judgment (see Is. 14:9,15; Mic. 4:1,3).

Paul's Concept of Wrath: *Wrath Is a Position*

In Paul, there is a gathering up of both these Old Testament ideas and the adding of a new concept as well.

Paul speaks numerous times of "the wrath of God," but he never speaks of God's being angry (see Rom. 1:18; Eph. 5:6; Col. 3:6). This indicates a basic difference in Paul's idea of the wrath of God. *It does not come as a direct punishment as the result of God's being angry, but rather, is the position into which one places himself through rebellion against God!* Paul understands that

---

1. R.C.H. Lenski, *The Interpretation of St. Paul's Epistle to the Romans* (Minneapolis: Augsburg Publishing House, 1961), 90.

God designed the world in such a way that the soul who sins must die (see Ezek. 3:18). *The moral order contains the punishment within it for the sin committed.* When God created the universe, He shined His image into it. His holy character is contained within the creation, so that cause and effect are an indisputable part of the moral universe. Disobedience causes one to reap what he sows regardless of his belief to the contrary.

When the laws of agriculture are unheeded, the harvest fails. When the laws of architecture are broken, the building collapses. When the laws of health are disregarded, the body sickens. The punishment is inherent in the sin, just like the child, who having been warned of the hot stove, insists in his rebellion on touching it. The pain of disobedience is the punishment contained within the act of disobedience. This is Paul's development of the Old Testament concept of God's wrath.

It is from this very wrath that God Himself provides mankind salvation through Jesus Christ. Into the awfulness of man's sin comes God's love—and that love of God, by an act of unbelievable grace, lifts man out of sin and saves him from the wrath, the inevitable punishment of sin, he deserves!

Man Cannot Plead Ignorance

Because what may be known of God is manifest in them, for God has shown it to them. For since the creation of the world His invisible attributes are clearly seen, being understood by the things that are made, even His eternal power and Godhead, so that they are without excuse (Romans 1:19-20).

There are three ways God has revealed Himself to mankind: through the Law, through the gospel, and through creation. If a man does not have the opportunity to hear the gospel, he still has occasion to see the image of God that He *epiphanied* (shined forth) into the created order.

Paul says, "Look at the world—see how it is constructed." The sinner, therefore, is without excuse. He cannot plead ignorance. This tells us something about God and our responsibility to Him. He has shown us His invisible attributes in the things that are clearly seen, so "that they are without excuse." This is why man's sin always leads him to destruction.

The sinner's sin is that knowing this, he did not look to God, but to himself for his remedy:

Because, although they knew God, they did not glorify Him as God, nor were thankful, but became futile in their thoughts, and their foolish hearts were darkened (Romans 1:21).

The word for "darkened" is *skotos* and means "confused." Man, in his confusion, parades his ideas, opinions, and speculations as the standard of life instead of the will of God. The sinner lives in a self-centered universe instead of a God-centered universe. This is the core of sin.

The result of self-centered living is idolatry:

Professing to be wise, they became fools, and changed the glory of the incorruptible God into an image made like corruptible man—and birds and four-footed animals and creeping things (Romans 1:22-23).

The word for "image" is *eikon* and is the term that shows how idolatry developed. A worshiper must have an image. Man traded God's image for his own corruptible image and then debased himself further in the worshiping of animals. This is why idolatry has been true of every false religion and non-religion since the fall of man. When a man makes an idol and brings sacrifices to it, it is always his purpose that his own aims and desires might be fulfilled. He whose worship is self-centered, not God-centered, does it for his own sake, not God's glory. Notice that Paul begins idolatry with man, then birds, then four-footed animals, and finally, creeping things. Idolatry always leads on a downward slide.

In conclusion, these verses have taught us that the very essence of sin is to put self in the place of God. Sin is self-worship, no matter what form it may take; and sin is, no matter how one may look at it, idolatry, pure and simple, because the very essence and basis of sin is man worshiping himself instead of God; therefore, sin in the final analysis is idolatry.

The only recourse left for God is to give man over...

Chapter 5

Given Over by God

*T*he wrath of God brings us immediately to the next set of verses focusing three distinct times upon the type of person sin produces. There are three passages that begin with the phrase, *"God gave them up."* Let us examine them:

*Therefore **God also gave them up to uncleanness**, in the lusts of their hearts, to dishonor their bodies among themselves, who exchanged the truth of God for the lie, and worshiped and served the creature rather than the Creator, who is blessed forever. Amen. For this reason **God gave them up to vile passions**. For even their women exchanged the natural use for what is against nature. Likewise also the men, leaving the natural use of the woman, burned in their lust for one another, men with men committing what is shameful, and receiving in themselves the penalty of their error which was due. And even as they did not like to retain God in their knowledge, **God gave them over to***

a debased mind, to do those things which are not fitting; being filled with all unrighteousness, sexual immorality, wickedness, covetousness, maliciousness; full
of envy, murder, strife, deceit, evil-mindedness; they
are whisperers, backbiters, haters of God, violent,
proud, boasters, inventors of evil things, disobedient to
parents, undiscerning, untrustworthy, unloving, unforgiving, unmerciful; who, knowing the righteous judgment of God, that those who practice such things are
deserving of death, not only do the same but also approve of those who practice them (Romans 1:24-32).

Three Downward Steps Into *Real* Trouble

First, we must understand the dynamics of free will.
God gave man free will, and God has bound Himself to
respect that freedom of choice. In effect, God has
given man the ability, if he so chooses, to rebel against
Him and go his own way.

Before man there stands an open choice. This must
be so, for without free choice there can be no love, no
goodness, as neither can be forced and still be real.
Therefore, if we are to be truly human, we must have
the freedom deliberately to reject God.

Second, because God honors man's choice, He reluctantly relinquishes His hold on man, and this is
what we mean by the term "given up by God." In the
original it is the word *paradidomi* and is better translated "given over" rather than "given up." If it were

epididomi, it would mean "given up," as if God were to say, "I give up on you; go to hell." But that is not the term. The word Paul used denotes a reluctant loosening of the grip, rather than a forceful abhorrence. In the act of giving man over, God is actually revealing His mercy in granting a temporary stay of self-execution.

When we speak of God giving persons over to something, we must never see emotional anger or hatred in it (as in the Mosaic Period) or even immovable justice (as in the Prophetic Period). Instead, there is sorrow and regret, as demonstrated in a husband who having done all he can for his wife allows her to go her own way (as demonstrated in the Hosea/Gomer relationship), or as evidenced in a father who can go no farther with his rebellious son and permits him to waste himself in prodigal living yet still continues to love him.

Third, there is judgment in this "giving over" by God. It is not God's angry judgment; *it is instead the inherent judgment that sin brings upon itself!*

Sin begets sin. This is the most tragic judgment of sin. The more a man sins, the easier it is to sin. This is not to say that God is punishing the man who sins; it is to say that *man is bringing judgment upon himself by his sin.* The old rabbis are often quoted as saying that, "Every fulfillment of duty is rewarded by another; every transgression is punished by another." Because

Israel indulged in idolatrous tendencies, "God...gave them up to worship the host of heaven" (Acts 7:42a). Because man, Paul says in Romans 1:18-23, wanted to worship self after he knew God, God gave him over to the even more vile practices listed in Romans 1:24-32.

It is the awful responsibility of free will that it can be used in such a way that in the end it is destroyed, and a man becomes the very slave of sin. Sin is always a lie, because the sinner thinks that his sin will make him happy, although it always ruins him and those closest to him. Sin ruins a person totally—both in this life and in the life to come!

A question I am often asked is, "Did God send AIDS? Is AIDS a direct judgment from God upon homosexuals?" My answer to this dilemma is no. AIDS is the inevitable consequence of sin, as all sickness is. The judgment is inherent in the sin.

In understanding Paul's concept of being given over by God, we must understand that God has the power to prevent man from sinning; but if He were to exercise this power, it would destroy man. Evil is pulling on one side; man is in the middle. If God were to pull on His side, man would be ripped asunder and the image of God in man would be destroyed. Therefore, God, in allowing man the freedom of his own will, *reluctantly relinquishes His grasp* on man, permitting him to choose that which will eventually destroy him, even giving him the strength to rebel against God.

Given Over to Uncleanness

Therefore God also gave them up to uncleanness, in the lusts of their hearts, to dishonor their bodies among themselves, who exchanged the truth of God for the lie, and worshiped and served the creature rather than the Creator, who is blessed forever. Amen (Romans 1:24-25).

The key word in this passage is "lusts." *Epithumia* is the Greek word and means "feeling upon," or "forcing one's feelings upon another," which is what lust is. Lust leads to "uncleanness" (*akatharsia*), which is the opposite of *catharsis* (a clean heart). In the Greek there is a very practical application of this term: backed up bowels resulting in unhealthy blood. Uncleanness leads its followers into sexual immorality causing people to "dishonor their bodies among themselves" and "change the truth of God for the lie."

Akatharsia epithumia is passionate, unclean lust. It never finds permanent satisfaction and must explore other types of sin in order to express and fulfill itself. Returning to the subject of AIDS: One of the earliest entertainers who died of AIDS was asked by a reporter why he went into a lifestyle of homosexual promiscuity. He replied that after so many women one tires of regular sex and must explore other ways to satisfy one's self.

This entertainer gave everyone who heard him the testimony of *akatharsia epithumia*. He had been given over to uncleanness that resulted in his premature death.

Aristotle spoke of lust as "a reaching out after pleasure." The Stoics defined lust as "a reaching out after pleasure which defies all reason." Lust is *the passionate desire for forbidden pleasure*. It is a kind of insanity that makes one do things that he/she would never have done if this desire had not taken away his/her sense of honor and self-respect.

The downward earmark of every degenerating society in the history of the world is lust. Back in the 60's when "Free Love" was fostered upon our society, I was a professor in a famous college in California. During the weekends, there were group sex sessions involving not only students but even faculty members, all engaged in "Free Love Sessions." They were nothing more than orgies.

Those who were involved in this shameful spectacle were those who espoused the popular "God is dead" theory of the time. I thought of Paul's statement here in Romans, that because they did not glorify God in His creation, but insisted that creation was a product of evolution, they professed themselves to be wise, and instead, became fools, dishonoring their bodies among themselves through unbridled lusts.

I taught a comparative religions course at this college. My classroom guests were yogis, witches, occultists, and popular leaders of various religions. Many of the leading gurus of the day came and lectured my students. In all my dealings with these revered persons, *I did not find a single one whom I believed to be sincere in his or her beliefs.* All of them were in it for two things: sex and money. This leads us to the next giving over...

Given Over to Vile Affections

> *For this reason God gave them up to vile passions. For even their women exchanged the natural use for what is against nature. Likewise also the men, leaving the natural use of the woman, burned in their lust for one another, men with men committing what is shameful, and receiving in themselves the penalty of their error which was due* (Romans 1:26-27).

The words translated "vile affections" are *pathe atimias* and mean dishonorable passions. Unlike *epithumea*, which means to desire upon, this term refers to desires that are abnormal. "Vile affections" are at their root unacceptable to God because they are passions that are not permitted even within marriage. They are passions of dishonor.

Paul immediately describes these dishonorable passions by describing the unnatural practice of homosexuality: "For even their women exchanged the natural use for what is against nature. Likewise also the men, leaving the natural use of the woman, burned in their lust for one another, men with men committing what is shameful."

I don't care for the phrase "natural use" because it sounds as if women and men are to be *used* in the sexual experience. It is not an expression in keeping with our vernacular today. Paul is simply referring to *natural order* here. God created Adam and Eve, not Adam and *Steve*. Homosexuality upsets the natural order of God's plan for mankind.

Paul now returns to his previous thought, that sin contains its punishment within itself: "And receiving in themselves the penalty of their error which was due." The sin of homosexuality, Paul says, contains its punishment inherently, that is, the receiving into one's body the penalty due. This reinforces what I earlier said about AIDS and, of course, includes *all sexually transmitted diseases*, whether homosexual or heterosexual.

Was Paul Exaggerating?

Paul sounds like an overwrought moralist who is hysterically exaggerating the degree of moral degeneracy in his day, doesn't he? He has been accused, by those ignorant of the practices in the ancient Roman Empire, of stretching the truth to fabrication. The opposite is actually the case—Paul did not exaggerate the extent of vice in his day. On the contrary, he used restraint in his language here. He lived in a day of unparalleled immorality. This is easily shown by statements made by his contemporaries. I am indebted to William Barclay's excellent volume, *Romans*, for the paragraphs that follow.[1]

1. Barclay, *Romans*, 48-51.

The General Morals of the Era:

The poet Propertius said, "I see Rome, proud Rome perishing...the victim of her own prosperity. Ours is an age of moral suicide...when things seem out of control, and in the background, a man could hear the mocking laughter of the gods."

Seneca, a contemporary of Jesus and Paul, and uncle of Caesar Nero, the Mad Emperor, wrote, "it was an age stricken with the agitation of a soul no longer master of itself."

Tacitus, in his *History of Rome*, observed: "I am entering upon the history of a period, rich in disasters, gloomy with wars, rent with seditions, savage in its very hours of peace...All was one delirium of hate and terror, slaves were bribed to betray their masters, freedmen their patrons. He who had no foe was destroyed by his friends."

Suetonius remarked, "No day passed but someone was executed. It was an age of sheer, utter terror."

Livy agreed. "Rome could neither bear its ills nor the remedies that might have cured them."

Virgil: "Right and wrong are confounded..."

Tacitus said, "Crime became the only antidote to boredom—the greater the infamy, the wilder the delight."

The Sexual Debauchery of the Era:

Juvenal: "To find a single virgin in all of Rome is unbelievable."

Historical fact: *There had not been one single case of divorce in the first 520 years of the republic's history!* The first divorce was recorded in 234 B.C. "But now," said Seneca, "women were married to be divorced and divorced to be married." Rich women dated their years by the names of their husbands! **One high-born lass had eight husbands in five years.**

The typical Roman lady was "girt like Venus with a golden girdle of vice," wrote Clement of Alexandria. (The goddess Venus, adored by young women, made nymphomania respectable in ancient Rome.)

The Empress Messalina, wife of Claudius, "often left the royal palace at night and served in a brothel for the sake of sheer lust!"

The caesars themselves were morally bankrupt. Fourteen of the first fifteen emperors were homosexual or bisexual. Caligula was a brazen pedophile. A harem of young boys accompanied him on all his trips!

The Wealth of Rome:

All of this degeneracy was supported by unparalleled luxury. Never in the history of the world had wealth been so highly concentrated in one place. Juvenal said, "A luxury more ruthless than war broods over Rome. No guilt or deed of lust is lacking *since Roman poverty disappeared*...Money, the nurse of debauchery, sapped the sinews of the age with foul luxury" (emphasis mine).

It was an age so weary with ordinary things that it craved any new sensation.

The Emperor Caligula, while Palestine and other provinces starved in famine, sprinkled the floor of the circus arena with gold-dust instead of sawdust! In the public baths of Rome, hot and cold water ran from *silver faucets.*

Consider the parallels between ancient Rome and modern America. We are bored and our young people continually crave any new sensation. They are spoiled, even with more games to entertain them than ever before in man's history. Homosexuality is fast becoming accepted as an alternative lifestyle. Our crime rate has accelerated at such a pace that our states have run out of prison space and it isn't safe to go for an evening walk in even moderate-size towns. Our national conscience has been seared to the point that a majority of Americans now favor the practice of abortion that has claimed over 30,000,000 of our unborn citizens. Our society has become increasingly rude and impolite, and neighbors are much less friendly than they were even a decade ago.

Given Over to a Reprobate Mind

And even as they did not like to retain God in their knowledge, God gave them over to a debased mind, to do those things which are not fitting (Romans 1:28).

The Living Bible paraphrases verse 28 this way:

So it was that when they gave God up and would not even acknowledge Him, God gave them up to doing everything their evil minds could think of.

There is no other passage in Scripture that so clearly shows what happens to a man when he forgets God. It is not so much that God sends judgment on him; it is that he brings judgment upon himself. When a man leaves God out, he becomes a certain kind of man—a marked man. The remainder of Romans chapter 1 tells some of the characteristics of a marked man:

Being filled with all unrighteousness, sexual immorality, wickedness, covetousness, maliciousness; full of envy, murder, strife, deceit, evil-mindedness; they are whisperers, backbiters, haters of God, violent, proud, boasters, inventors of evil things, disobedient to parents, undiscerning, untrustworthy, unloving, unforgiving, unmerciful; who, knowing the righteous judgment of God, that those who practice such things are deserving of death, not only do the same but also approve of those who practice them (Romans 1:29-32).

Those who are described in these verses are less than purely human; they are debased. Indeed, the person who casts away God from his life not only loses godliness, he loses manliness too. Let's look at the chief words in this text.

1. *Unrighteousness* (Strong's #93)—This word is *adikia* and is the opposite of the word for justice. Justice is giving to God and others their due,

but an unrighteous person robs God and others by erecting an altar to himself that excludes all else.

2. *Fornication* (#4202)—This is the word *porneia* from which the word pornography is derived. It means the active, deliberate desire to corrupt and injure. It denotes unlawful sexual relationships of all kinds, not only sex between two unmarried persons.

3. *Covetousness* (#4124)—This word is *pleonexia* and means rapacity; the cursed love of possessing. It is the spirit that pursues its own interests to the deliberate disregard of others.

4. *Maliciousness* (#2549)—This word, *kakia*, is where the Spanish get their word "caca." We all know what this means! And this is how we should view maliciousness, which is the degeneracy out of which all sins grow; viciousness; essentially bad. A malicious person is one who always turns to the worse.

5. *Envy* (#5355)—*Phthonos* is resentment of others who are better than myself.

6. *Murder* (#5408)—This word, *phonos*, not only refers to the deed of violence itself, but the anger and hatred that produces the deed. Man regards the deed. God sees the intention.

7. *Strife* (#2054)—*Eris* refers to contention born of envy, jealousy, and ambition.

8. *Deceit* (#1388)—The word *dolos* is the quality of the tortured and twisted mind that cannot act straightforwardly and honestly, but must stoop to underhanded methods to get its own way.

9. *Malignity* (#2550)—This word is *kakoetheia* and refers to a living cancer growing in someone! This is akin to our word "malignant." It literally means an evil-naturedness or the spirit that always puts the worst construction on everything. It always thinks the worst of others.

10. *Whisperers and Slanderers* (#5588,#2637)—This phrase, *psithuristes, katalos,* refers to people with slanderous tongues. The whisperer gets his hearer in a corner and destroys another's character. The slanderer trumpets his "information" abroad to everyone.

Each of the above characteristics denotes the reprobate or debased mind to one degree or another. Paul says that because men did not like to retain the knowledge of God, but insisted on that which their vile affections led them unto, God reluctantly relinquished His control of these persons and gave them over to whatever evil their minds could think up.

We will not look at them a great deal, but the general characteristics of reprobate persons follows. They became haters of God, insolent (despiteful), proud (arrogant), boasters (braggarts), inventors of evil, disobedient to parents (which means apathetic to parental authority), without understanding (senseless), covenant breakers (breakers of agreements), without natural affection (*astorgos*, which means without familial love), and implacable and merciless (pitiless).

Upon these types of persons Paul adds the most condemning verse in all of literature:

Who, knowing the righteous judgment of God, that those who practice such things are deserving of death, not only do the same but also approve of those who practice them (Romans 1:32).

It isn't difficult to see a tragic parallel between Paul's day and ours. The famous historian, Arnold Toynbee, once said, "*No nation has ever survived the loss of its gods.*"

Here, Paul gives us a terrible picture of what happens when men deliberately banish God from their lives. Rome perished for this very reason and so will every man and every nation that does not return to God.

Chapter 6

Taking Wrong Advantage of God's Mercy

herefore you are inexcusable, O man, whoever you are who judge, for in whatever you judge another you condemn yourself; for you who judge practice the same things. But we know that the judgment of God is according to truth against those who practice such things. And do you think this, O man, you who judge those practicing such things, and doing the same, that you will escape the judgment of God? Or do you despise the riches of His goodness, forbearance, and longsuffering, not knowing that the goodness of God leads you to repentance? But in accordance with your hardness and your impenitent heart you are treasuring up for yourself wrath in the day of wrath and revelation of the righteous judgment of God, who "will render to each one according to his deeds": eternal life to those who by patient continuance in doing good seek for glory, honor, and immortality; but to those who are self-seeking and do not obey the truth, but obey unrighteousness— indignation and wrath, tribulation and anguish, on every soul of man who does evil, of the Jew first and also of the Greek; but glory, honor, and peace to every- one who works what is good, to the Jew first and also to the Greek. For there is no partiality with God (Ro- mans 2:1-11).

The Jews and Their Failure: *Responsibility Not Privilege*

In the first chapter of Romans, Paul condemned the Gentile or "heathen" world for their debased behavior. With every word of denunciation the Jew had gleefully agreed. "Yes! God will blast those wicked Gentiles out of existence at the end-time! He will make them fodder for the furnace of hell!" Here, Paul addresses the Jews in their "abominable self-righteousness."

The Jew never dreamed that he was under a similar condemnation as "the Gentile dogs." He thought he held a privileged position in the sight of God. But in this passage Paul says in no uncertain terms that *the Jew is just as guilty as the Gentile,* and that being a Jew by birth will not exempt him from God's wrath.

It is difficult for us to believe that any person could think that he is essentially better than anyone else, but many first century Jews actually believed this! The only modern comparison many Americans can relate to is the superiority whites felt toward blacks, especially in the South. Thank God, this form of racial prejudice is being eradicated from our society, but it was a great problem while I was growing up. I was raised in Georgia, and I can tell you that not all whites felt they were better than blacks; I never bought that lie, but many of my contemporaries did. Not all the Jews in Paul's day believed they were superior to Gentiles, but many, if not most, of them did. It was part of their religion and culture.

Let me give you several quotes from this period preserved in the rabbinical sayings of the Talmud:

"God loves Israel alone of all the nations of the earth."

"God will judge the Gentiles with one measure, and Israel with another."

"All Israelites will have part in the world to come."

Note this one in particular:

"Abraham sits beside the gates of hell and does not permit any wicked Israelite to go through."

Now, it is true that God did love Israel in a special way above the other people groups of the world through His special *covenant* love with Abraham and his seed. There is a unique word for His love for Israel, *chesed*, which refers to His merciful lovingkindness to them rather than the *agape* type of love. God "*agaped*" all peoples, as the Law, Psalms, and the Prophets showed, but this is something the Jew forgot. The Jew believed that everyone was destined for judgment except himself!

In Justin Martyr's *Dialog with Trypho*, published in the first century, the Jew Trypho said:

> "They who are of the seed of Abraham according to the flesh shall in any case, even if they be sinners and unbelieving and disobedient towards God, share in the eternal Kingdom."

This false belief was not based upon any special goodness that would keep the Jew immune from the wrath of God, *but simply the fact that he was a Jew!*

Against this Paul brought three points:

1. Paul bluntly told the Jews that they were taking advantage of, and trading on, the mercy of God.

2. Paul exposed the erroneous belief that the Jew regarded the mercy of God as an invitation to sin rather than an incentive to repent.

3. Paul reproved them with the truth that there is no favoritism with God.

We will look at these three points under separate headings.

Taking Advantage of Mercy

Or do you despise the riches of His goodness, forbearance, and longsuffering, not knowing that the goodness of God leads you to repentance? (Romans 2:4)

In verse 4 he uses three great words:

Goodness (*chrestotes*)—This word means beautiful deed. Therefore, the Jews looked upon God as being always essentially *chrestotes* (kind) in this treatment of them, whether they were right or not. Of course, God was more pleased with good behavior, but He would always be kind or nice to Israel. Therefore, they took advantage of the kindness of God.

Forbearance (*anoche*)—This word means truce, or cessation of enmity for a limited period. Forbearance is essentially giving one a chance to escape deserved punishment.

Paul says that the Jews were being given such a chance by God, but they were adulterating this forbearance of God and turning it into a license to sin. They were trading on the mercy of God. A day will come when the limit of God's mercy will be used up and God's wrath will follow.

Longsuffering (*makrothumia*)—The word means great feeling and shows patience with people. *Makro* means large or great, in contrast to *mikro*, which means small (as in microscope), and *thumia* means feeling. Chrysostom called it:

"The characteristic of the one who has it in his power to avenge himself upon an enemy who has done him wrong, but does not use it."

It is the spirit of one who has power to destroy the one who hurts and insults him, but who in patient mercy does not. It would be like an enemy who has wronged you for years and then shows up in your yard deserving your punishment, but you show mercy instead.

The Jews had for so long trafficked on God's mercy that they had fooled themselves into believing that God could not punish them—that they were especially immune to His wrath. He had been patient with them for so long that they felt entitled to it; they wrongly believed their relationship with Abraham provided special exemption for them as a people.

This vague, undefined hope of immunity has been a flaw in God's people of every age. It is a tragic, universal blindness. Even people who don't know God have the feeling judgment could never happen to them, but the Jews went even further. They openly claimed exemption from God's wrath and traded on His mercy.

We could liken their attitude to that of the often unfaithful husband who continues in adultery, expecting the ongoing, unconditional forgiveness of his spouse. After she has suffered all she can endure, this type of husband is frequently surprised by the divorce suit she brings against him. Because she had forgiven him many times, he disbelieved in eventual justice until she refused to take him back anymore.

How many do you know who do the same thing today in their relationship with God? They refuse to adjust their lifestyles according to His clear instructions, taking advantage of His forgiving nature. "Do not be deceived," Paul warned, "God is not mocked" (Gal. 6:7).

Mercy Is *Not* an Invitation to Sin!

The second point the Apostle makes is that God's mercy is not an invitation to sin, but an incentive to repent: "Don't you know the goodness of God is intended to lead you to repentance?" he asks (Rom. 2:4b paraphrased).

Heine, the German philosopher, once said that he was not worried about the world to come. Someone asked him why and he replied, nonchalantly, "Oh, God will forgive. It's His business to forgive." Forgiveness, however, is never presented in the Scriptures as God's *duty*, but always as His *gift*. A gift is a freewill present, not an obligation. God would be absolutely just had He never even offered forgiveness, but chose instead to judge His rebellious creature, man.

There are only two possible reactions to forgiveness. The first reaction is to realize how we have hurt the other and gratefully receive the forgiveness, purposing never to wrong that one again. The second reaction is to repeat the hurtful offense over and over, trading on the fact that we will be forgiven over and over.

It is one of the most shameful things in the world to trade on forgiveness, but that is precisely what the Jews in Paul's day were doing.

God's loving forgiveness is not meant to make us feel that we can sin and get away with it; it is meant to break our sinful hearts in love so that we will never want to sin again!

This is the true purpose of God's mercy and the only proper response to His forgiveness.

No Favoritism With God

Who "will render to each one according to his deeds": eternal life to those who by patient continuance in doing good seek for glory, honor, and immortality; but to those who are self-seeking and do not obey the truth, but obey unrighteousness—indignation and wrath, tribulation and anguish, on every soul of man who does evil, of the Jew first and also of the Greek; but glory, honor, and peace to everyone who works what is good, to the Jew first and also to the Greek. For there is no partiality with God (Romans 2:6-11).

This is the third argument the Apostle makes to the Jews: *There are no favored individuals in God's economy,* and no people group enjoys a "most favored nation" status with Him. There is no partiality with God, Paul declares, but tribulation and anguish will come upon the soul of *every man* who does evil—Jew or Greek.

How does this square with the scriptural teaching of Israel as God's covenant people? What about particular individuals who received unique callings from God?

We can answer these questions by agreeing that, yes, there are nations, groups, and individuals who are *selected to perform special tasks,* but there are no nations, groups, or individuals who are picked out for **special privilege.**

The renowned poet Milton once said, "When God has some great work He gives it to His Englishmen." History has *not* backed up his boast, however; but even if it were true, it would only affirm what we just said. Notice that Milton spoke of "some great work" which, of course, denotes special task or responsibility, not special privilege.

The whole of Jewish religion in Paul's day was based upon the belief that Jews held a position of special blessing and privilege in God—that Yahweh loved Israel more than He loved other peoples. This was not true. Israel's special place was in the area of responsibility, not privilege; performance, not position. They were to be His "kingdom of priests," but they sorely failed (Ex. 19:6). Only 400 years before the Messiah came Yahweh declared to Israel: " 'I have no pleasure in you,' says the Lord of hosts, 'nor will I accept an offering from your hands' " (Mal. 1:10).

The Jews' belief that God would not punish them because they were the *chosen ones* was grossly mistaken, as history shows. The Jews have been one of the most oppressed peoples in the history of the world. From the days of Pharaoh, Nebuchadnezzar, Sennacherib, and the Caesars until most recently under the insanity of Stalin and Hitler, the Jews have suffered the scourge of the nations. This evidences the true meaning of "chosenness." If God has selected you for some special purpose, He won't let you get by with anything!

"...Whom the Lord loves He chastens" (Heb. 12:6a). When the Lord selected Paul for apostleship He said, "For I will show him how many things he must suffer for My name's sake" (Acts 9:16).

Back in the days when I was studying at a Lutheran seminary, not a great many years after World War II, my roommate, Klaus Koch, and I became good friends. Klaus, as you may have guessed, was German. He came from a wealthy family who lost everything due to the ravages of war. Klaus came to America in order to become a Lutheran minister, a dream he has since fulfilled. Decades ago in seminary, our dorm room was the site of many interesting discussions on a wide range of issues. One day the subject turned to the recent war and the terrible devastation that occurred in Nazi Germany as a result of Allied Forces' bombs. I momentarily forgot with whom I was speaking and re-marked that Germany got what she deserved because the Germans had allowed that horrible monster, Hitler, to deceive them into believing they were a spe-cial race whereas all races are actually the same.

Klaus was a big man, in fact, about half a foot taller than I am and a good 40 pounds heavier. After I made my remark, Klaus crossed the room in a flash and peer-ing down over me looked straight into my eyes and asked, "And so, Cottle, you don't think what happened in my country could happen in *yours*?" Then he pointed out to me, and quite strongly I might add, that

Germany was the birthplace of the Reformation and that the German people were easily beguiled by Hitler due to the mistaken notion that they enjoyed a special status with God due to their rich religious heritage.

Germany made the same mistake in this century that the Jews made in Paul's.

Let me bring this down to where we live. Have you noticed an attitude of superiority among American Christians? Is there any prouder group of people than Pentecostals and Charismatics? Let the reader beware!

Faith or Works?

The discussion of favoritism leads into a related subject. What is the proper relationship between faith and works? The problem arises from misunderstanding the New Testament. Paul's writings stress that God saves men by faith apart from works. James tells us that faith without works is dead.

This problem of faith and works has plagued every generation of true believers. Augustine and Pelagius, Luther and Erasmus, Whitefield and Wesley, and on down to the present day the Church has waged a not so holy war within itself. The Reformers themselves battled one another over it to lesser degrees. Martin Luther, for example, remarked that he was going to use the letter of James to start his fire. He did not include it in his German translation of the Greek New Testament questioning its canonicity over this supposed "contradiction."

John Calvin, on the other hand, wisely affirmed James as canonical.

Today there are theologians who contemptuously wave aside a religion that stresses the importance of good works as being out of touch with the New Testament. *Nothing could be further from the truth.* James said, "Faith without works is dead" (Jas. 2:20), and Paul affirmed that, "God will settle with each man according to his deeds" (Rom. 2:6 paraphrased).

To Paul, a faith that does not express itself in deeds of love is a travesty. The fruitless faith is a parody of true faith. It is not faith at all. Paul agrees with James and does not contradict him. Paul's theology stresses that the only way you can see faith is through deeds of love. Paul always used the phrase *ek pisteos*, which means "up, out of faith." His problem with works concerned religious activity that does not proceed from faith, or what we could simply refer to as "dead works."

It is often argued that Paul taught that all that matters is faith, while James taught that all that matters is works. This is a caricature of both of the apostles. Paul was against using works as a means of justification, but spoke of good works as something that naturally takes place as a result of salvation (see Eph. 2:8-9; Eph 2:10). James spoke of works as something that naturally follows faith (see Jas. 2:18). There is really no contradiction between the two at all. Both men taught that true faith precedes the works it produces. *There can be no such thing as a faith that does not express itself in deeds of love, and there can be no such thing as deeds of love that are not the product of faith!*

Works and faith are inseparable. How else can God judge a man except by his deeds? The Christians of our day who profess faith without a corresponding lifestyle are making the same mistake the Jews made in Paul's day—they are taking wrong advantage of God's mercy.

Chapter 7

Three Ways God Will Judge Mankind

or as many as have sinned without law will also perish without law, and as many as have sinned in the law will be judged by the law (for not the hearers of the law are just in the sight of God, but the doers of the law will be justified; for when Gentiles, who do not have the law, by nature do the things in the law, these, although not having the law, are a law to themselves, who show the work of the law written in their hearts, their conscience also bearing witness, and between themselves their thoughts accusing or else excusing them) in the day when God will judge the secrets of men by Jesus Christ, according to my gospel (Romans 2:12-16).

The Gentiles and Their Failure: *The Unwritten Law*

As we begin our study of this passage, I must make something clear: The King James Version, which is my favorite one, is not inspired as far as all the punctuation is concerned. At this point in the letter, we have evidence of an excited Paul striding up and down in his room as he dictates to his secretary, Tertius, what he is saying here. (See Romans 16:22.)

This is a "problem passage" due to a long parenthesis, what scholars call an *anacoluthon*, which makes it difficult to understand the main thought of the paragraph. (The other *anacoluthon* in Romans is 5:12-[13-17]-18.) If we read the passage and skip over the parentheses, we will be able to understand the thought better. Therefore, as both Moffatt and Dodd suggest, we will omit verses 13-15 and read verses 12 and 16 for the main thought:

For as many as have sinned without law will also perish without law, and as many as have sinned in the law will be judged by the law ... in the day when God will judge the secrets of men by Jesus Christ, according to my gospel (Romans 2:12,16).

Now we can add verses 13-15 in order to form a perfect explanation of this main thought. Notice that the New King James Version observes the *anacoluthon* by enclosing these verses in a parenthesis:

(For not the hearers of the law are just in the sight of God, but the doers of the law will be justified; for when Gentiles, who do not have the law, by nature do the things in the law, these, although not having the law,

are a law to themselves, who show the work of the law written in their hearts, their conscience also bearing witness, and between themselves their thoughts accusing or else excusing them) (Romans 2:13-15).

Reading this passage in this manner helps us understand how God will judge the Gentiles who never knew the Law or heard the gospel. In Chapter 6 we saw how Paul condemned the Jews because they accepted the privileges associated with being God's special people but refused the responsibilities of such a position. Now, certain Gentiles might say that it was right for God to punish the privileged Jews, but that God should not hold the Gentiles responsible because they had no opportunity to know the Law and did not know any better; they simply did what came natural. In answer to such an objection, Paul gives us two great principles:

1. A man will be judged by what he had opportunity to know.

2. Even those who do not know the written Law have an unwritten law within their hearts.

God Is a Just Judge

When I was a young seminarian, one of the favorite topics of discussion concerned how God will judge mankind. We not only debated this matter in class, but also stayed up all hours arguing among ourselves this important subject. How will God judge the heathen who never heard of Jesus? How will He deal with children who died before the age of accountability? How will He judge the Jews both before and after the coming of Christ? These questions not only trouble young "theologs," they come up frequently in Sunday schools and Bible classes.

Paul gives the answer in this marvelous letter to the Romans. I can sum it up this way: *God will judge every man by the highest and the best that he knew.* God, Paul stresses, is just and will not judge anyone unjustly. This echoes Abraham's rhetorical question, which he put to the Lord: "Shall not the Judge of all the earth do right?" (Gen. 18:25c) Study this passage with me and see if you come to the same conclusion.

> *For as many as have sinned without law will also perish without law, and as many as have sinned in the law will be judged by the law ... in the day when God will judge the secrets of men by Jesus Christ, according to my gospel (Romans 2:12,16).*

"*For as many as have sinned without law will also perish without law....*" The Law God gave Moses will not be the criterion by which He judges the Gentiles who lived and died before Christ came. How will they be judged? They will be judged in accordance with the way they obeyed the unwritten law within their hearts:

> *For when Gentiles, who do not have the law, by nature do the things in the law, these, although not having the law, are a law to themselves, who show the work of the law written in their hearts, their conscience also*

bearing witness, and between themselves their thoughts accusing or else excusing them) (Romans 2:14-15).

How will Gentiles who lived and died since Christ came be judged? *By the same criterion!* They will be judged as to how they obeyed the unwritten law within their hearts. Paul says that the Gentiles have *conscience,* and if they obey their conscience, they will be saved. Having just said this, however, let me be quick to point out that due to depravity, there is no one who obeys his conscience. The fact remains, no matter how unlikely, that it is theoretically possible that there will be people in Heaven who were never exposed to the Law or the gospel, simply because they obeyed the unwritten law within their hearts.

Every person will be judged by his response and faithfulness to the highest and best that it was possible for him to know. If he has been true to the highest and best that it was possible for him to know, then a just and merciful God will not judge him on the basis of something higher!

A leader in one denomination heard this truth and exclaimed with all sincerity, "Thank God! There is no need for a missions department in our church." I shuddered when I heard him make that statement because the likelihood that someone will be always and entirely true to his conscience is highly unlikely, although, as I have said, it is possible in theory. But this does not release us Christians from the responsibility of evangelism.

As a general rule, mankind needs to hear the gospel due to the fall and the *personal violation of conscience* which every man experiences (Rom. 3:23). There are, in fact, no fewer than six reasons why we must preach the gospel to every creature:

1. Our Sovereign commands it.

    > *And He said to them, "Go into all the world and preach the gospel to every creature"* (Mark 16:15).

    Who was this Person issuing the Great Commission? None other than our risen Lord, who is *kurios* (Sovereign Lord, Absolute Ruler). How can we claim obedience to our King otherwise? The fact that He alone commands it should be reason enough for our doing it.

2. The Word demands it.

    > *Go therefore and make disciples of all the nations, baptizing them in the name of the Father and of the Son and of the Holy Spirit* (Matthew 28:19).

    There is no such thing as an evangelical who does not profess to believe the Word of God. There it is, clear as day. The Scriptures demand that we herald the good news to all nations.

3. Agape compels it.

    > *For the love of Christ compels us, because we judge thus: that if One died for all, then all died* (2 Corinthians 5:14).

Jesus designated loving one's neighbor as the second greatest commandment. How could someone who has come to know Jesus not long to share Him with others, especially those who have never heard of Him?

4. The Spirit empowers it.

> *But you shall receive power when the Holy Spirit has come upon you; and you shall be witnesses to Me in Jerusalem, and in all Judea and Samaria, and to the end of the earth* (Acts 1:8).

The Holy Spirit was not sent just to make us better worshipers or to help us know God more intimately. He does this in our lives, it is true, and much, much more; but one of His primary purposes, if not *the primary purpose*, is to empower believers to share Christ even unto "the uttermost parts" (KJV).

5. God's purpose includes it.

> *For since, in the wisdom of God, the world through wisdom did not know God, it pleased God through the foolishness of the message preached to save those who believe* (1 Corinthians 1:21).

Preaching is the one redemptive function of man. There is nothing humans can do to better their society more than preach the gospel. I believe this so strongly that I predict the end of any society that excludes preaching. God purposed that through preaching the gospel, people will receive the faith He requires for salvation:

> *For "whoever calls on the name of the Lord shall be saved." How then shall they call on Him in whom they have not believed? And how shall they believe in Him of whom they have not heard? And how shall they hear without a preacher?* (Romans 10:13-14)

6. Expediency requires it.

> *And this is eternal life, that they may know You, the only true God, and Jesus Christ whom You have sent* (John 17:3).

Faith in Christ is the best way to gain life and salvation because accepting Him gives *zoe* life now as well as hereafter. The Hassidic Jew of our day struggles to obey the Law in his own energy; the uninformed islander beholds the wonders of creation and ponders the infinite Being who made it without even knowing His name. The true Christian is the only person on the planet who has the present joy of salvation bubbling within him. The Christian can live a life that is pleasing to God because Christ lives it in and through him. All others fail because they attempt it in their own energy.

The Instinctive Knowledge of Right and Wrong

The second great principle of this text, as stated earlier, is that those who don't know the written Law (or the gospel) have an unwritten law within their hearts. Some have referred to this as "the instinctive knowledge of right and wrong."

The Stoics were popular in Paul's day, and many of them lived in Rome. They were known for stressing certain inviolable laws of the universe, which man broke at his own peril. The Stoics observed that there were unwritten laws of health, which one broke to his own hurt, and laws of morality, which one broke to his own pain. They referred to these inviolable laws as *PHUSIS*, or the laws of nature. (It is interesting that *phusis* is the root word for "physics.") They urged men to live *KATA PHUSIN*, or according to nature, that is, *do the moral and healthy thing within your own environment.*

Nearly all great thinkers have recognized this as a cornerstone of human life. Socrates taught that all knowledge is innate; and therefore, in order to make a man good, one need only educate him, that is, lead his innate knowledge out of him so that he will be able to grasp it with his conscious mind. (The word "educate" comes from two root words: *ducare*, which means "to lead or draw," and *e*, which means "out." Education is the process of drawing out the knowledge innate within man.) Aristotle, the direct student of Plato, who was the direct student of Socrates, demonstrated this principle when he said, "The cultivated and free-minded man will behave as being a law to himself." Aristotle said this because the man who brings knowledge from within himself will live by it. Plutarch agreed: "Who shall govern the governor? Law, the king of all mortals and immortals...not written on papyrus rolls or wooden tablets, but in his own reason within the soul...."

Paul picks up this idea, already well known in Rome and to his readers, and "Christianizes" it here in this text. He says that in the very nature of every man there is implanted an innate, inherent, instinctive knowledge of what he ought to do. Paul makes this instinctive knowledge the criterion by which God will judge the uninformed in the last day.

Three Large Classes of People

How should Christians view their world today in terms of the pending Day of Judgment? What is the Christian's responsibility in it?

I believe that there are basically three large classes of people in the Christian worldview of mankind:

1. Those who have heard the gospel.

2. Jews who have the Law of God.

3. Those who have neither the written Law (non-Jews), nor have heard the gospel (non-hearers).

Each class of people will be judged by the highest and the best it was possible for them to know.

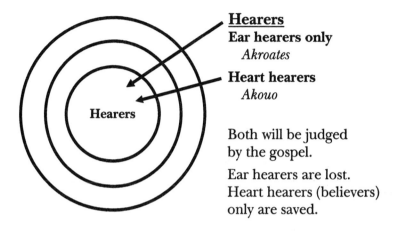

Hearers
Ear hearers only
Akroates

Heart hearers
Akouo

Both will be judged
by the gospel.

Ear hearers are lost.
Heart hearers (believers)
only are saved.

Diagram A

The Hearers

There are two kinds of hearers: *akouo* (pronounced: ah KOO oh) and *akroates* (pronounced: ah KRO ay taas). The *akouo* hearers are "heart hearers"; the *akroates* hearers are "ear hearers."

The "ear hearers" are referred to in James 1:22, "But be doers of the word, and not hearers [*akroates*] only, deceiving yourselves." This means they hear the Word with the natural ear, but not the heart.

The *akouo* people are those who hear and believe. They are referred to in Matthew 11:15; Mark 4:23; Revelation 2:7,11; et al. One of the clearest examples of heart hearers is Romans 10:17, "So then faith comes by *hearing* [*akouo*], and hearing by the word of God."

The heart hearers are saved; the ear hearers are not. Both will be judged by the highest and the best it was possible for them to know: the gospel.

The Jews

There are those who have not heard the gospel, but have heard the Law. They don't place their trust in Jesus, but in the Law. In a biblical sense there are a lot of people who come under this category because they don't trust Jesus, but their own efforts. They are practical Jews.

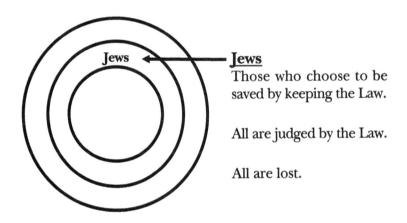

Jews
Those who choose to be saved by keeping the Law.

All are judged by the Law.

All are lost.

Diagram B

Paul enlightens us concerning the state of the Jews when he says, "For circumcision is indeed profitable if you keep the law; but if you are a breaker of the law, your circumcision has become uncircumcision" (Rom. 2:25). Notice the first part of this verse: "*For circumcision is indeed profitable....*" The word for "profitable" is *sumpheron* (the word "ferry" comes from here) and means to bring together (just as a ferry transports someone from one place to another). If a Jew kept the Law, he would be brought together with God. God did not give the Law to condemn Israel, but as a means by which Israel could relate to Him. However, because no one kept the Law, it did not profit them. The Law was good, but weak through the flesh (see Rom. 7:12; 8:3). This is why circumcision is a matter of the heart, rather than the flesh, and why no one will be justified by the deeds of the Law (see Rom. 2:28-29; 3:19-20). Still, we must never make the mistake some have made, suggesting that the Law was faulty; we were the ones at fault. If anyone could keep the Law, it would ferry him to God.

What is the result then? The Law brought the knowledge of sin, rather than the intended salvation. This is because the Law depends upon man and man is incapable of keeping the Law. Therefore, the Jew is in need of the gospel because "it is the power of God to salvation for everyone who believes, for the Jew first and also for the Greek" (Rom. 1:16). God is just to judge the Jew by the Law, but to be judged by the Law inevitably to be condemned. It isn't the Law's fault; it's man's fault because of sin. There is only one verdict: GUILTY!

Those Who Have Neither Law nor Gospel

These are the "people groups" who do not have the gospel or the Law. We should not call them "heathen"

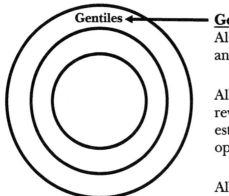

Gentiles

Also called "Nations" and "Heathen."

All are judged by natural revelation—or the highest and best that they had opportunity to know.

All are lost.

Diagram C

because that has become a misnomer. They are simply the *ethnoi* or the ethnic groups throughout the world. These are the Gentiles who have not heard of Jesus.

The people groups, as we have seen in our text, will be judged by *natural revelation* because it is the highest and the best it is possible for them to know. Natural revelation is the revelation of nature—an ordered cosmos (Rom. 1:20). However, it also might include the so-called great religions *of man* (!), namely: Hinduism, Taoism, and their offshoots, as well as Islam and others. These are *natural* in that they are born in the soul of man and do not come from God as do Judaism and Chrisitianity. God promises "eternal life to those who by patient continuance in doing good seek for glory, honor, and immortality" (Rom. 2:7). Due to the fall, however, the people groups of the world are not able to live up to "patient continuance in doing good" because "there is none who does good, no, not one" (Rom. 3:12). They will be judged by natural law and fall short of the glory of God.

In each situation God stands just in every case because He will only judge a person according to what he or she knows and has had opportunity to know. The hearers will be judged by the gospel; the Jew by the Law; the non-Jew who has never heard of Jesus by natural revelation. None is exempt from God's demand of holiness. None is exempt from God's provision of love. *But all are declared guilty!* The only group of people who will be saved are the *akouo hearers* (those who hear and believe the gospel of Christ with the heart).

Chapter 8

The Faithfulness of God

O: *What advantage then has the Jew, or what is the profit of circumcision?*

P: *Much in every way! Chiefly because to them were committed the oracles of God.*

O: *For what if some did not believe? Will their unbelief make the faithfulness of God without effect?*

P: *Certainly not! Indeed, let God be true but every man a liar. As it is written: "That You may be justified in Your words, and may overcome when You are judged."*

O: *But if our unrighteousness demonstrates the righteousness of God, what shall we say? Is God unjust who inflicts wrath?*

P: *Certainly not! For then how will God judge the world?*

P: *For if the truth of God has increased through my lie to His glory, why am I also still judged as a sinner?*

P: *And why not say, "Let us do evil that good may come"?—as we are slanderously reported and as some affirm that we say. Their condemnation is just* (Romans 3:1-8).

These verses constitute a very well reasoned and difficult argument by Paul. He raises objections and then answers them as though he were carrying on an argument with an imaginary objector. Perhaps you noticed the letters "O" and "P" before each verse in our text. "O" stands for the imaginary objector and "P" stands for Paul. Please go back and carefully read the text again before we attempt to disentangle the passage and bring out the basic thoughts.

The Jews Special Position With God

O: *What advantage then has the Jew, or what is the profit of circumcision?*

P: *Much in every way! Chiefly because to them were committed the oracles of God* (Romans 3:1-2).

The word for "oracles" is *logia* and not only refers to the *dabar Yahweh* (the Hebrew term for the commandments of God), but also to the special position Israel had with God by virtue of their covenant. The Jews reading this passage would agree with Paul. They had a special position with God that no other people had, but they would disagree as to the implication. The Jew believed he held a position of special *privilege*; Paul believed the Jew held a position of special *responsibility*.

The special position of the Jew is that to him God had committed the *logia tou Theou*, the oracles, or better, Word of God, which is a reference to the Decalogue (the Ten Commandments). These oracles, or the Word Yahweh spoke to Israel from Mount Sinai, were commandments Israel was to obey, not just a privilege to enjoy (see Ex. 20:1; 24:3,8). God essentially said to them, "You are My special people, not so you can do as you please, but that you must do what I please. You are a special people; therefore, you must live a special life."

Special choice by God always brings special responsibilities to God!

Three Basic Ideas About Israel

Paul gives, in embryonic form, his three basic concepts about Israel which permeate all his writings. They are a part of the very basis of Romans—one of the foundation stones of the epistle and are contained within verse 3:

For what if some did not believe? Will their unbelief make the faithfulness of God without effect?

The three basic ideas from this verse are:

1. *God had justly condemned Israel.*

Israel had special position and responsibilities, but they failed in them; therefore, they stood under God's wrath. (For his development of this theme, refer back to 2:1-29 and especially notice verses 1,25,27,29.) It is the principle of Romans that the greater a man's privileges the greater his responsibilities and *the greater his condemnation when he fails.*

2. *Not all Jews were unfaithful.*

There was a "faithful remnant" to whom God was still faithful in keeping the promises He had made to the Patriarchs. These were His "true Israel."

3. *God's rejection of Israel is not final.*

Because Israel failed God and was rejected, a door was opened to the Gentiles and through them God would bring the Jews back into the fold. The Gentile and the Jew were to become one in Christ.[1]

This presents a very important step of progress—a switch in the divine economy for the salvation of the world God so loved. Please notice the reverse of strategy which occurred:

---

1. Note: These thoughts are fully developed by Paul in chapters 4,9,10,11. In my third volume of this series of four books, these passages will be treated under the title, *The Church: The True Israel.*

1. Jesus and His disciples preached primarily to Jews in order to win them and Gentiles.

2. Paul preached primarily to Gentiles in order to win them and Jews.

It is highly improbable that Jesus and His disciples ministered directly to the Gentiles. In all of the Gospels there are only two, perhaps three, incidents of Jesus ministering to the ethnics. In Matthew 8:5-13 Christ ministered to the Roman centurion; in Mark 7:24-30 He ministered to the Syro-Phoenician woman; in Mark 5:1-20 He delivered the demoniac of Gadara, about whose race there is a question that cannot be definitely answered. The centurion and the Syro-Phoenician both came to Jesus unbidden, and unlike any Israelites to whom Jesus ministered, each received a commendation from Him for their faith! We must keep in mind that in both cases these Gentiles sought Jesus out and pressed their way upon Him—He did not go to them.

Jesus specifically instructed His disciples not to go to "the Gentiles...but go rather to the lost sheep of the house of Israel" (Mt. 10:5-6). Their scope of ministry was "the cities of Israel" (Mt. 10:23). Years later the commission of Peter was to the circumcision, so his focus remained upon his natural brethren (see Gal. 2:7). Throughout his entire ministry, Peter remained faithful in his calling as the "apostle to the Jews" except for the time "the Spirit bade [him] go" to the household of

Cornelius, the Italian. Cornelius, however, was not reflective of the ordinary Gentile because he was a "God-fearer," as the proselytes to Judaism were called. (Gentiles who abandoned their polytheism for monotheism were called "God-fearers" as a term of honor.) Even though Cornelius was a God-fearer, Peter was called on the carpet by the brethren in Jerusalem for having gone to a Gentile's home to preach the Messiah (see Acts 11:1-18).

Why were Jewish believers focused on Israel in the earliest days of the Church? They understood that God's method was one of reaching the world through redeemed Israel, failing to comprehend the significance of the phrase "the uttermost parts of the earth" given by their Lord during His last post-resurrection appearance (see Acts 1:8-9). They mistakenly believed that until all of Israel was redeemed, there was little use in going into all the world.

In Paul, however, there came a basic change of method, which scholarship has titled *the Gentile Mission*. Paul sees that the Jews have shunned their responsibility, and therefore takes the gospel to the Gentiles with the expectation that through redeemed Gentiles God will eventually save Jews! In fact, this is the only way the Jews can be saved today—through the ministry of the Church.

In Paul, God's original strategy was reversed. Instead of Jews evangelizing Gentiles as God had originally intended, the Gentiles saved through Christ become the real Jews who then evangelize those who were not true Jews—the members of the nation of Israel who had rejected their Messiah. This evangelization process is still in progress. Peter preached primarily to Jews in order to win Gentiles also; Paul preached primarily to Gentiles in order to win Jews also.

The modern Church can learn a lesson from this. Strategies may fail and need changing; the purpose, however, always remains the same. When methods of evangelism are not productive, more fruitful means of reaching people must be employed. Through Paul, the strategy was reversed, but the purpose remained unchanged. In the Old West, during the days of the Pony Express, it often happened that an animal collapsed from exhaustion. This did not stop the mail because a new pony took its place. The mail kept going out; and so the Church must adjust and drop the old exhausted methods in order to keep the message going out.

Two Great Universal Truths

In the balance of this chapter, Paul presents two great universal truths:

1. *The basic root of sin is disobedience.*

   The beginning of the Jews' problems and the root of Israel's sin was disobedience to the known law of God. Paul earlier explained this in Romans 1:21: "Because, although they knew

God, they did not glorify Him as God, nor were thankful, but became futile in their thoughts, and their foolish hearts were darkened." The basic root of sin is disobedience. Pride set the minds of the Jews against the will of God and that is sin. If there were no disobedience, there would be no sin.

2. *Once a man has sinned, he displays amazing ingenuity in justifying his sin.*

It has been characteristically true of mankind since the fall that when he sins, he seeks to justify himself through rationalization rather than humble himself and confess his sin. The Jew argued that his sin provided more opportunity for God to reveal His grace; therefore, his sin was serving the purpose of God. What a twisted argument! It is clearly the reasoning of a reprobate mind, a mind to which evil has become good and good has become evil.

William Barclay commented, *"When a Man does sin, the need is not for ingenuity to justify the sin, but for humility to confess it in penitence and in shame."*[2]

---

2. Barclay, *Romans*, 50.

Chapter 9

Can a Person Go Too Far to Be Saved?

*W*hat then? Are we better than they? Not at all. For we have previously charged both Jews and Greeks that they are all under sin. As it is written: "There is none righteous, no, not one; there is none who understands; there is none who seeks after God. They have all turned aside; they have together become unprofitable; there is none who does good, no, not one. Their throat is an open tomb; with their tongues they have practiced deceit; the poison of asps is under their lips; whose mouth is full of cursing and bitterness. Their feet are swift to shed blood; destruction and misery are in their ways; and the way of peace they have not known. There is no fear of God before their eyes." Now we know that whatever the law says, it says to those who are under the law, that every mouth may be stopped, and all the world may become guilty before*

God. Therefore by the deeds of the law no flesh will be justified in His sight, for by the law is the knowledge of sin (Romans 3:9-20).

The Christless World

In the previous chapter, we saw how Paul insisted that the Jew held a special position in the economy of God to save His lost world in Romans 3:1-8. Remember the "imaginary objector" in that passage? Guess what? He is still with Paul and asks in verse 9: "What then? Are we better than they?" This is to say, "If what you have just said is so, does it mean that the Jews are better than other people who are not Jews?"

Paul's answer is a decisive NO! "No, in no wise" (KJV). The Jews are not better than the Gentiles because all men are "under sin," both Jew and Gentile alike. (See verses 9-18 for Paul's elaborate description of universal human depravity.)

There are two very important expressions in this passage. The first is "under sin" (v. 9), and the second is "unprofitable" (v. 12).

Under Sin

The Greek says *hupo harmartian*. *Hupo* means in the power of or under the authority of. The centurion said his soldiers were *hupo emauton*, or, "under me" (Mt. 8:9). A schoolboy was *hupo paidagogon*, or under the authority of his pedagogue. A slave was *hupo zugon*, or under the yoke of his master. *Hamartia* is the word for "sin." It literally means "to miss the mark." So man, apart from Christ, is under the command, under the authority, and under the control of sin. He is helpless to escape it. *A sinner cannot **not** sin.* It is an impossibility because he is under its dominion. The sinner misses the mark every time; then rebellion comes and the sinner, in vain hopes of justifying himself, redraws the mark to something he can hit. This redrawing of the bulls-eye, then, becomes the essence of apostasy.

Unprofitable

Man under wrath (and please remember that wrath is not an emotion or possession, but a position) becomes *unprofitable*. This is the word *achreioo* and means "rendered useless." This word was used in ancient literature for milk gone sour, which in that time was useless for any purpose. Man, apart from Christ, is a sour and useless thing. Man as he is portrayed in the first three chapters of Romans is human nature gone sour! This word is also used for savourless salt, which Jesus said was good for nothing (Mt. 5:13).

Stringing Pearls

In verses 10-18 Paul uses a common Rabbinic teaching method that we refer to today as proof-texting. The word for this is *charaz* and literally means "stringing pearls!" Paul now begins proof-texting the fact that fallen man is under the dominion of sin and soured.

He strings together six quotes from the Old Testament that buttress his point of the sinner's valuelessness. (If you would like to compare these they are Psalm 14:1-3 in verse 12; Psalm 5:9 in verse 13a; Psalm 140:3 in verse 13b; Psalm 10:7 in verse 14; Isaiah 59:7-8 in verses 15-17; Psalm 36:1 in verse 18.)

These "pearls" describe three things about man apart from Christ: his character, his confession, and his conduct.

The essence of the sinner's *character* is 1) *ignorance*: "There is none who understands" (v. 11a); 2) *indifference*: "There is no one who seeks after God" (v. 11b); 3) *crookedness*: "They have all turned aside (v. 12a); 4) *unprofitableness*: "There is none who does good, no, not one" (v. 12b).

The essence of the sinner's *confession* is 1) *destructiveness*: "Their throat is an open tomb" (v. 13a); 2) *deceitfulness*: "With their tongues they have practiced deceit; the poison of asps is under their lips" (v. 13b-c); 3) *malignancy*: "Whose mouth is full of cursing and bitterness" (v. 14).

The essence of the sinners *conduct* is 1) *oppressiveness*: "Their feet are swift to shed blood" (v. 15); 2) *injuriousness*: "Destruction and misery are in their ways" (v. 16); 3) *implacability*: "And the way of peace they have not known. There is no fear of God before their eyes" (vv. 17-18).

These are the characteristics of a person apart from God. There is nothing in the universe more evil or depraved than fallen human nature. Paul knew this—he admitted it—yet he never gave up on a single evil human being. He always believed every man to be in the reach of saving grace. Paul never underestimated the sin of man, but he also never underestimated the grace of God.

Like Paul, I believe in original sin and human depravity, yet I do not despair of human beings. I proclaim the gospel of Christ that can transform human nature. As awful as fallen man is, the power of God unto salvation is much, much more wonderful!

A great old saint said one day, "My memory is failing, but there are two things I never forget. First, that I am a great sinner and second, that Jesus Christ is a greater Savior."

A young minister had been preaching for months without success. He became badly discouraged and wanted to leave the ministry. He went to visit his pastor, a man he greatly admired, and told his tale of woe: the people were hardened, the congregation unruly, and sinners mocked his message. It is said that after awhile D.L. Moody looked at his young friend and said, "Okay. Go ahead and quit. Your hearers are too sinful to be saved. Their sin is bigger than God's grace." With that the young man broke as he realized how he had limited God. Tears fell to the floor and the burden lifted. He returned to his work ready to carry on until God gave the answer.

Man without Christ is bad, but he is never too bad to be saved. The wondrous hymn, "The Love of God," says it better than I can:

> The love of God is greater far
> Than tongue or pen could ever tell.
> It goes beyond the highest star
> And reaches to the lowest hell.
>
> The guilty pair bound down with care
> God gave His Son to win.
> His erring child He reconciled
> And pardoned from his sin.
>
> O, love of God, how rich and pure!
> How measureless and strong!
> It shall forevermore endure
> The saints' and angels' song.

Finally, we conclude this first major section of Romans concerning man under wrath with 3:19-20:

Now we know that whatever the law says, it says to those who are under the law, that every mouth may be stopped, and all the world may become guilty before God. Therefore by the deeds of the law no flesh will be justified in His sight, for by the law is the knowledge of sin (Romans 3:19-20).

The Living Bible does a very good job with these two verses:

So the judgment of God lies very heavily upon the Jews, for they are responsible to keep God's laws instead of doing all these evil things; not one of them has any excuse; in fact, all the world stands hushed and guilty before Almighty God. Now do you see it? No one can ever be made right in God's sight by doing what the law commands. For the more we know of God's laws, the clearer it becomes that we aren't obeying them; His laws serve only to make us see that we are sinners.

What does this say? It says three things. Simply put: 1) The Law speaks to the Jews, and its basic function is that every mouth is stopped and the whole world is guilty before God; 2) Nobody can ever get into a right relationship with God by doing good works; 3) All this provides a recognition of what sin is so the sinner can turn from sin to the Savior.

We are now ready to proceed to the second great section of Romans...

Chapter 10

The Righteousness of God

*B*ut now the righteousness of God apart from the law is revealed, being witnessed by the Law and the Prophets, even the righteousness of God, through faith in Jesus Christ, to all and on all who believe. For there is no difference; for all have sinned and fall short of the glory of God, being justified freely by His grace through the redemption that is in Christ Jesus, whom God set forth as a propitiation by His blood, through faith, to demonstrate His righteousness, because in His forbearance God had passed over the sins that were previously committed, to demonstrate at the present time His righteousness, that He might be just and the justifier of the one who has faith in Jesus (Romans 3:21-26).*

"But Now…"

In this passage we reach a major turning point in the Book of Romans. Until now the Apostle has diagnosed man's disease; he now examines God's cure. Paul's theme has been the sin of man and God's wrath against it; he now proclaims righteousness, not wrath; grace, not rebellion. The discussion of righteousness begins in 3:21 and continues to the end of chapter three.

Someone said, "Man's extremity is God's opportunity." This was never so true as at this point in Paul's letter. The final climactic conclusion of the preceding section about man's condition is 3:19b, "All the world [is] guilty before God." It is repeated again like an awful echo in 3:23, "For all have sinned and fall short of the glory of God."

This chapter's text begins with a great sigh of relief: *"But now...." A new day is dawning, says Paul; God is offering His righteousness to placate His wrath against man's sin. I believe that this is the greatest passage of Scripture in all the Word of God. If I were permitted only one book it would be the Bible, if only one letter it would be Romans, if only one passage it would be Romans 3:21-31. Everything needful for salvation is contained right here."*

In this final chapter of Volume I, we will do three things with this magnificent and extremely difficult passage:

1. Discuss the righteousness of God (verses 21-26).

2. Deal with some of the great concepts of this passage.

3. Pick up the last three arguments of Paul (verses 27-31).

Righteousness Is a New Position

In Chapter 3 of this book, "Righteousness and Justification," we examined the Greek word for "righteousness": *dikaioo*. We saw that all Greek verbs that end in "oo" (ah-owe) do not mean to *prove* a person or a thing to be something, or even to *make* a person or a thing something. Instead they always mean to *treat, account,* or *reckon* a person to be something. In this word it means to accept, treat, reckon, or declare a person to be just as if he had never sinned.

As we also saw in Chapter 3, justification is the act of God by which the sinner is given this new standing of righteousness. Justification itself does not change the sinner's nature—regeneration and sanctification do that; but justification changes God's view of the sinner and puts him in a new account in which he is treated as though he were righteous, actually declaring him to be righteous. Justification is a *forensic* term, that is, a legal term, which comes out of a court of law. The evidence against the sinner is irrefutable, but then the judge declares the sinner not guilty. God does what is improper in any human court of law—He acquits the criminal of his crimes.

It is on this new position of righteousness that Paul places his emphasis in 3:21-22:

> *But now the righteousness of God apart from the law is revealed, being witnessed by the Law and the Prophets, even the righteousness of God, through faith in Jesus Christ, to all and on all who believe. For there is no difference* (Romans 3:21-22).

In this phrase Paul does not use merely *dikaioo* but *dikaiosune Theou*—the righteousness of God.

The Righteousness of God

First, in verse 21, Paul describes the righteousness of God *negatively*. He says, "the righteousness of God without the law is revealed." Although Paul's understanding of the righteousness of God is in complete harmony with the Old Testament revelation of God in the Law and the Prophets (which Paul will show in detail in 4:1-25), the righteousness of God is "without the law," that is, it does not consist of a Pharisaical keeping of the minute rules and regulations of the Jewish law.

Second, in verse 22, Paul describes the righteousness of God *positively*. He shows that it comes by "faith in Jesus Christ," or as the King James Version correctly translates it, the "faith *of* Jesus Christ," which is given to us. The preposition "of" is the translation of the *genitive of possession* and means the faith that belongs to Jesus Christ. It is not our faith that saves us, but His faith which is given to us! Paul declared that saving faith is itself "the gift of God, not of works, lest anyone should boast" (Eph. 2:8-9). The righteousness of God is received by believing, not achieving; trusting, not doing.

Three Facets of the Righteousness of God

Being justified freely by His grace through the redemption that is in Christ Jesus, whom God set forth as a propitiation by His blood, through faith, to demonstrate His righteousness, because in His forbearance God had passed over the sins that were previously committed, to demonstrate at the present time His righteousness, that He might be just and the justifier of the one who has faith in Jesus (Romans 3:24-26).

In this passage Paul describes three facets of God's righteousness:

1. Its *FORM*—A Judge's Gift
2. Its *BASIS*—A Substitute's Sacrifice
3. Its *PURPOSE*—A Divine Vindication

1. The Form of Righteousness

The form of righteousness is a judge's gift: *"Being justified freely by His grace..."* (3:24). The phrase "by His grace" denotes a free gift. God, who is "the Judge of all the earth," freely justifies sinners who place their faith in Christ's redeeming work by giving them His righteousness (see Gen. 18:25). Righteousness takes the form of a judge's decision by a pronouncement of acquittal.

Paul's teaching shocked the Jews to their very core because their interpretation of these Scriptures declared just the opposite:

He who justifies the wicked...[is] *an abomination to the Lord* (Proverbs 17:15).

...I will not justify the wicked (Exodus 23:7).

Paul says, on the contrary, that this is exactly what God does! He justifies the wicked; we don't have to get good enough for God to love us. Is this really a contradiction? NO! God justifies the wicked only *because He has first satisfied the demands of justice in His own Son on the cross.*

When a person really believes this, it changes his whole relationship with God. He is no longer plagued by his sins, living in terror, separated, estranged, and alone. Like a penitent, brokenhearted child, the sinner comes before a holy God who treats him not like an angry judge, but like a loving Father! Jesus illustrated this truth in the parable of "The Prodigal." The father took back his wayward son and treated him like a son, not a servant. He embraced him, fed and clothed him with the best he had, and called him his son. He was telling him, by word and deed, to become what he was—A SON. (See Luke 15:11-32.)

Sadly, many Christians have not been taught sufficiently this truth in their churches. They live in defeat, always doubting their position in Christ, approaching God as timid, backward servants instead of coming to Him as trusting sons.

2. *The Basis of Righteousness*

The basis of righteousness is a substitute's sacrifice: "*...through the redemption that is in Christ Jesus*" (Rom. 3:24b).

The word for "redemption" is *apolutrosis* from *apo*, which means "from, back" and *lutrosis*, which means "to purchase, buy, or pay a price." Redemption occurred when God bought us back from the slave market of sin through a substitutionary sacrifice of the blood of His Son.

3. *The Purpose of Righteousness*

To demonstrate His righteousness, because in His forbearance God had passed over the sins that were previously committed, to demonstrate at the present time His righteousness, that He might be just and the justifier of the one who has faith in Jesus (Romans 3:25b-26).

It was "to demonstrate [declare—KJV] His righteousness" of character now ("at the present time") because He had "passed over the sins that were previously committed" in the past. This vindicates God for showing His large-heartedness, the truce (cease fire), when He winked at men's sins before Christ died since He judged their sins at the cross. The Jews, as we saw in Chapter 6, had traded on God's mercy and had taken wrong advantage of His passing over of their sins. What this passage means is that God showed Himself to be *at the same time* both a God who 1) deals faithfully with sin and 2) saves sinners who put their trust in Jesus.

What about those who died before Jesus offered Himself? What happened to them? The answer is that if they lived up to the highest and the best that they knew, they descended into the upper compartment of *Sheol/Hades* at death into the region known as Paradise (Abraham's Bosom). They were kept in that place of relative comfort, separated from hell-fire (*Gehenna*) by a great gulf, awaiting the coming of the Messiah. The first sins Christ expiated on the cross were the sins of these very souls who had died in faith not receiving the promise (see Heb. 9:15). It is outside the scope of this book to delve into this at length, but suffice it to say that all those who died in faith before Calvary were included in Calvary's benefit.

Highlights of This Passage

Now we will go deeper into this passage by considering some of its great concepts.

Faith in Jesus Christ (Rom. 3:22)

Jesus' faith is given as a gift to us. It is not our faith (it does not originate in us). We direct the faith we receive towards God. We receive the righteousness God owns through the faith Jesus owns and gives to us.

The Glory of God (3:23)

What is the glory of God? There are two answers.

First, the glory of God refers to man's original state as created in the likeness of God. Spiros Zodhiates comments:

"When we read in Romans 3:23 that they come short of the glory of God, it means that they are not what God intended them to be. They lack His image and character."[1]

God has called us "to His eternal glory" (1 Pet. 5:10). This is the glory man had with God before the fall, when he was "the image and glory of God" (1 Cor. 11:7).

The second way to consider "the glory of God" is by translating the Greek word *doxa* into its Old Testament equivalent, the Hebrew word *cavodh*. This Hebrew word literally means "heavy, weighty." It is used, for example, of a king who had a "heavy sword" or many fighting men in his army. *Cavodh* refers to the weightiness of God's presence.

The Jews referred to this visible splendor of God as *shakan* from which the word "Shekinah" is derived. The Shekinah was the luminescent cloud by day and the golden pillar of fire by night. *Shakan* means to cover over as the cloud covered over the wilderness tabernacle. But the *shakan* did not actually cover the tabernacle or the people. Do you know what it covered? The Shekinah covered the *cavodh*, which was hidden in or under it. The Glory, the *cavodh Yahweh*, is the heavy, awesome presence of Yahweh! Man was not permitted to see the Glory in his unredeemed state. This is why the Shekinah covered it. Not even Moses, the

---

1. "Lexical Aids to the New Testament" *Hebrew-Greek Study Bible* (Chattanooga: AMG, 1984). See study on *doxa*.

friend of God, was permitted to see the Glory. He was granted to see only the residue after the Glory had passed (see Ex. 33:18). (Most of the time we hear Shekinah and Glory combined into "the Shekinah Glory." It is not correct to equate the Shekinah and the Glory as synonymous. The former was a covering for the latter.)

As a young preacher, I prayed for the Shekinah to fill our meetings. Later I came to realize that it wasn't the cloud I needed, but the glory hidden under the cloud. I now pray for the *cavodh*, the weighty presence and power of God, to fill my life and ministry. I have come to understand that in the truest sense of the word, I and other Christians are the Shekinah (*Shakan-Yah*), for His glory dwells in us (1 Cor. 3:16).

Grace (3:24)

Grace is the word *charis*, the undeserved favor of God, unmerited kindness shown to one unworthy. This word was often used for an act of kindness shown by a superior to an inferior. For Paul, it means the free, unmerited kindness of God to sinners.

Redemption (3:24)

This is the word *apolutrosis*, which we studied a few paragraphs earlier. It is a concept straight out of the ancient slave market. It originally meant to ransom a slave from bondage with the payment of money. Later this word was used for deliverance, in the general sense of the meaning of that term. The idea is that God in Christ provides deliverance from the guilt, power, and penalty of sin for those who trust completely in Jesus Christ.

Let me refer you to the Book of Hosea for an enlightening study of redemption. Hosea redeemed his unfaithful wife, Gomer, as a type of Yahweh's redemption of His faithless bride, Israel.

Propitiation (3:25)

The Greek word here is *hilasterion* and should not be rendered "propitiation." To propitiate means "to appease; to change from anger to love, from hatred to pleasure." But this is not what happened at Calvary. God did not change His mind about us, as though He had reconsidered His anger at our sin and decided He would not be upset anymore! Nor should we ever make the mistake that Yahweh was an upset deity whose Son placated and calmed Him by His bloody cross. This is a concept that is more at home among the idol worshipers throughout the world whose gods must be appeased through various human sacrifices than with the true God. It is true that Christ's offering pleased the Father and removed our guilt.

The Revised Standard Version has the word "expiation" here instead. Expiation *describes the annulment of sin, to flood or wash away.* God set forth Jesus to annul our sins, to set us free from sin's power, penalty, and guilt. But this, too, is an imperfect expression, though it is much better than propitiation.

The understanding of propitiation is that the perfect sin offering removed our guilt, while in expiation His offering removed our filth. Both of these have a measure of truth, but the third understanding of *hilasterion* is the clearest and, I believe, the best one.

The third understanding was given by the former monk turned reformer, Martin Luther. Luther rendered *hilasterion* as "mercy-seat," on the basis of his exegetical and etymological studies of the parent word of *hilasterion*, which is *hilasmos*. This word *hilasmos* is used in Hebrews 9:5 where it is correctly translated "mercy seat."

The Mercy Seat

The mercy seat was the golden lid of the Ark of the Covenant where the golden cherubim sat with their eyes on each other and their wings spreading out before them until they touched. This lid was rectangular and measured 47 inches long by 27 inches wide. Within it was the rod of Aaron, a pot of manna, and the tablets God gave Moses.

Every year on Israel's holiest day, *Yom Kippur*, the high priest carried the blood of the sacrificial lamb into the Holy of Holies and sprinkled it upon the golden lid, or the mercy seat.

There are three reasons why Luther used the word "mercy seat" in Romans 3:25, and they prove why Luther's translation of *hilasterion* is the best one:

1. This is the usual meaning of *hilasterion* in the Septuagint (the Greek Old Testament). This was the word the Jewish scholars used to translate *kapporeth* from the Hebrew text into Greek and means "the cap" or the cover of the Ark of the Covenant (the lid on top of the chest).

2. The setting in which *hilasterion* appears in the verse: "whom God set forth as a propitiation (*hilasterion*) by His blood...." Notice, "by His blood" immediately follows *hilasterion,* and the blood was sprinkled upon the mercy seat on Yom Kippur (the Day of Atonement).

3. In Christian literature outside the New Testament, *hilasterion* always means "a place" rather than an idea or something intangible. It is never used of an act or a deed.

What Paul is saying in all of this is simply that *the crucified Jesus has become for all the world, both Jew and Gentile, what the mercy seat was for Israel!* What was symbolically figured forth on the Day of Atonement in Israel was fulfilled completely in Christ Jesus. ***Christ on His cross is the one and only place where God fully shows His forgiving grace to men!***

Therefore, *hilasterion* literally means "the place of atonement" (at-one-ment) where man is reconciled to

God. *Hilasterion* means propitiation (KJV), expiation (RSV), and mercy seat (Luther).

The End of the Way of Human Achievement

Where is boasting then? It is excluded. By what law? Of works? No, but by the law of faith. Therefore we conclude that a man is justified by faith apart from the deeds of the law. Or is He the God of the Jews only? Is He not also the God of the Gentiles? Yes, of the Gentiles also, since there is one God who will justify the circumcised by faith and the uncircumcised through faith. Do we then make void the law through faith? Certainly not! On the contrary, we establish the law (Romans 3:27-31).

There are three arguments of Paul in the closing verses of chapter 3:

1. *If the way to God is to accept Jesus by faith, then all boasting in human achievement is gone.*

This truth applies to all merit systems of human endeavor, which endeavor is the basis of all false religions. But in particular Paul was addressing the ghost of his past—*Pharisaism* because it represented the finest of Jewish religion and Judaism was the best of all world religions prior to the cross since it had been instituted by God.

The Pharisees were a 6,000-member sect in Israel who committed their entire lives to obeying every word of scribal law. A Jew became a Pharisee, a set-apart one, by taking a solemn vow before three witnesses in which he promised, "I will give my life to keep every detail of scribal law." The basic premise of Pharisaism was:

> The Law contains the whole Word of God for every possible situation in every possible moment for every possible man, either explicitly or implicitly.

The scribes of ancient Israel gave their lives to extracting an infinite number of rules and regulations to govern every conceivable life situation. The Pharisees pledged their lives to keep every one of these regulations. For them all of the scribal laws were just as valid as the Mosaic Law, although Jesus referred to the scribal laws as the traditions of men, which make the Word of God of no effect (see Mt. 15:6; Mk. 7:13). Here is how the scribal laws developed:

1. The Ten Commandments
2. The 613 Mosaic Laws
3. The Mishna
4. The Gemara
5. The Palestinian Talmud
6. The Babylonian Talmud

The center of the Law is Deuteronomy 6:4-5: "Hear, O Israel: the Lord our God, the Lord is one...." This was called the *Shema*. All of the laws from the Mishna forward claimed to be based upon the *Shema*. This developed into the multiplication of legalism. The Babylonian Talmud, for example, contains 2,902 very large plates on which are written 1,302 civil laws, 785 ritual laws, and 815 family life laws!

Let me give another example. The fourth commandment is, "Remember the Sabbath day, to keep it holy" (Ex. 20:8). There are 24 chapters on how to keep the Sabbath in the Mishna, 64 1/2 full columns in the Palestinian Talmud, and 156 double pages in the Babylonian Talmud! One rabbi spent two and one-half years studying just one chapter of the Mishna's instructions on the Sabbath!

The important thing to keep in mind is that when the Pharisee did all of this, he actually believed he was putting God in his debt! The Pharisee kept a running ledger in his mind, a kind of profit and loss ledger, and every time he obeyed a law he made a mental entry on the credit side. A Pharisee came to the point of such obedience to scribal law that he honestly believed God owed him for his superior lifestyle *and actually became his servant, rather than his Master*!

Paul's position, indeed the whole of the Gospels and the New Testament, is the exact opposite of this. No man can ever work himself into a right relationship with God, let alone put God in his debt! Every person is a debtor to God, and every ground for self-justification and boasting is gone forever. "Where is boasting then? It is excluded. By what law? Of works? No, but by the law of faith. Therefore we conclude that a man is justified by faith apart from the deeds of the law" (Romans 3:27-28).

2. *The way to God is the same for Jew and Gentile.*

Paul's second point is the logical corollary to the argument the Jew raised. The Jew, in response to Paul's insistence on grace rather than works as the basis for acceptance with God, was, "Hey, your doctrine is great for Gentiles who never had the *Shema*. Let them be saved by faith, but what about the Jews who do know the Law?"

To answer this, Paul insists there is not one God for Gentiles and another God for Jews: "Or is He the God of the Jews only? Is He not also the God of the Gentiles? Yes, of the Gentiles also, since there is one God who will justify the circumcised by faith and the uncircumcised through faith" (Rom. 3:29-30). When Paul says, "There is one God," the Jew immediately thought of the *Shema* ("the Lord thy God is one"). It is this one God who saves both groups of people, Jew and Gentile, the same way: "By faith and...through faith" (Rom. 3:30).

3. *This does not nullify the Law, but strengthens it.*

Paul asks himself the question that he anticipates arising in his Jewish readers. "Do we then make void the law through faith?" (Rom. 3:31a) We might expect Paul to reply in the affirmative, but, indeed he responds with an emphatic no: "Certainly not! On the contrary, we establish the law" (Rom. 3:31). What does he mean by this?

Up to now the sincere Jew had tried to keep the Law because he was afraid of God. He feared the punishment he would suffer if he broke the Law. Now that day is gone forever, but not the keeping of the essence of the Law. *Only the reason for keeping it has changed.* Now a man is to keep the Law (that is, its intents, principles, and purposes, not the minute details) solely out of *love for God who gave the Law*, not out of fear of His wrath.

The effect of the change from law to grace is twofold:

1. It frees a man from terror, fear, and guilt (see Rom. 8:3).

2. It binds a man closer to God than ever before through love, not fear.

What we must understand about the Law from its inception is that the Law revealed the heart of God, His moral attributes and characteristics; and breaking the Law should be viewed as breaking God's heart, which those who love Him would never want to do. Because a person is justified by faith, he is free to obey the moral law of God because the power of sin, which held him in dominion, is forever broken. We do not access God by the Law, but by faith in Jesus Christ. He then writes His law upon our hearts and we live in accordance with His nature. This is the way "we establish the law" (Rom. 3:31). Thus we have been brought *from wrath to righteousness!* From God's NO to God's YES.

Epilogue

*I*n this first volume of our study on Romans, we traveled with Paul over a wide area of thought—all the way from the wrath of God, which is due all mankind for failure to heed conscience, natural law, and moral law, to the righteousness of God, which is the source of salvation by faith in Jesus Christ.

We began our study of Romans with an overview of the life of the greatest apostle of our faith. We saw how he was transitioned from Saul to Paul. We looked at the earliest Gospel, the *Kerygma*, and we recognized that all the written literature of the New Testament was preceded, informed, and shaped by it.

We looked at righteousness and justification and saw that although the effects of sin are great, the effects of righteousness are even greater. We learned from Paul that the only means of receiving righteousness is by faith alone.

In these pages, we studied the full biblical understanding of the wrath of God. We saw that wrath is first revealed in the Torah as an emotion. Then it is revealed in the prophets as a possession. Finally it is in Paul's writings as a position. We saw the true meaning of salvation, which is being delivered from the wrath of God and placed in a harbor, or refuge, of safety from the wrath we justly deserve. We understood that apart from Christ all hope of rescue from wrath is fruitless, but in Him our safety is assured.

We looked at what Paul meant by declaring that God gave mankind over to uncleanness and some of our race over to a reprobate mind. However, we also know that no one can go too far to be saved, no matter what depths of sin he plumbs. Because unsaved man is under wrath, God must judge him, and there are three ways God will judge mankind.

We looked at the faithfulness of God to Israel in spite of her unfaithfulness to Him. We saw that the way to God is the same for Jew and Gentile—through Jesus, our Saving Sacrifice! We saw Jesus presented as the actual Mercy Seat of God, the unchanging surety of salvation for all who come to God by Him. We concluded this volume by focusing on the grace of God and the wonderful effects this grace affords the believer.

This naturally leads us to consider the kind of life the believer enjoys as a result of the multi-faceted grace of God he experiences in union with Jesus Christ. The new life of the believer is the theme of Romans 5 through 8, as well as Volume II of this series. It is the author's intention for Volume II to be published in 1997.

Volumes III and IV are already planned for 1997 and 1998 respectively. These will address *The Church: The True Israel*, and *Ethics of the Kingdom*.

Other *exciting titles* by Dr. Ronald E. Cottle

ANOINTED TO REIGN

by Dr. Ronald Cottle.

In this insightful study of the life of David, Dr. Ron Cottle brings the skillful eye of a Hebrew and Greek scholar to bear on the Bible accounts of David's difficult ascent to the throne of Israel. He notes that David went through three "schools" of preparation for his reign, and reveals invaluable principles of leadership for us as we "train to reign" in fulfillment of our calling. This compelling book is a "must read" for every minister, serious student, and disciple following in the steps of Christ.

Paperback Book, 182p.
ISBN 1-56043-176-8
Retail $8.99